For Those with Little Dust

Pointers on the Teachings of Ramana Maharshi

For Those with Little Dust

Pointers on the Teachings of Ramana Maharshi

By Arthur Osborne

InnerDirections Publishing

Inner Directions Foundation
P.O. Box 130070
Carlsbad, California 92013
Phone: (760) 599-4075 • (800) 545-9118
www.InnerDirections.org

First Edition published 1987
Second Revised Edition 2001

Printed in Canada on recycled paper

Book & cover design by Joan Greenblatt
Drawing of Arunachala Hill by Sri Ramana Maharshi

ISBN: 1-878019-17-1
Library of Congress Catalog Card Number: 2001092490

To Sri Ramana Maharshi:

Such have I known,
Him of the Lustrous eyes, Him whose sole look
Pierced to the Heart,
Wherein the seed was sown
Of wisdom deeper than in holy book,
Of truth alone.
—from *Ramana Sat-Guru*, by Arthur Osborne

Table of Contents

Part III

Insights on the Spiritual Quest

Poems

"The ultimate Truth is so simple, it is nothing more than being in one's own natural, original state."
—Sri Ramana Maharshi

Foreword

Arthur Osborne was one of those rare individuals in whom an exceptionally keen intellect and an intensely introspective and poetic spirit were wonderfully integrated. From childhood, Arthur possessed an innate understanding of the unity that underlies all existence. This profound conviction nurtured his earliest aspirations and provided the spiritual foundation from which his entire life blossomed forth.

As a young man in Europe, he was attracted to the writings of the French philosopher, René Guenon, who intellectually confirmed for him the concept of "Oneness of Being." Arthur immediately felt the truth of this philosophy, which affirms that by realizing our true Self we also realize our identity with Absolute Being; but he had yet to experience it directly. When he began to read the original teachings of Bhagavan Sri Ramana Maharshi in the small booklet *Who am I?*, he was further strengthened in what he already felt to be true. However, only after receiving the "initiation by look" from Maharshi's luminous eyes did he directly experience "the depth of peace and an indescribable lightness and happiness" that began to awaken in him an awareness of the Self.

This initiation by look vitalized him and enabled him to actively pursue the path of Self-knowledge through the constant inquiry, "Who am I?" In following Ramana Maharshi's path, Arthur Osborne harmoniously balanced Self-inquiry, true devotion, and selfless service. He was a towering example of an ascetic living a family life. After the physical demise of Maharshi in 1950, Arthur began to write a number of articles and books in English that have spread the teachings of Ramana Maharshi throughout the world. He wrote a vivid portrayal of his guru's life entitled *Ramana Maharshi and the Path of Self-Knowledge*, and compiled his teachings in the book *The Collected Works of Ramana Maharshi*. He also compiled key passages of Sri Bhagavan's teachings, explaining them with intuitive comments when necessary, and published them in a book which has become a classic, *The Teachings of Ramana Maharshi in His Own Words*. Like a powerful magnet, these books have drawn earnest seekers to the path of Self-inquiry.

Arthur Osborne's love for Arunachala, the sacred hill in Tiruvannamalai, South India, that attracted Ramana Maharshi as a youth in 1896, was unique. Arunachala was his home, both physically and spiritually, even when obligations called him away. During the years he lived at Arunachala, he grew to be a gentle guide and inspiration for the spiritual aspirants nearby. Because of the deep devotion he felt for his guru, his great humility, and the steadfast way in which he pursued Self-Inquiry, many were attracted to him.

In 1964, fourteen years after Ramana Maharshi passed away, *The Mountain Path* was created. Both Arthur Osborne and I simultaneously felt the strong need to create a quarterly journal that would provide a forum for all authentic spiritual teachings, as well as a vehicle for the wisdom of Ramana Maharshi. Arthur Osborne, as editor, concerned himself with the literary content, and I became the managing editor, looking after the practical side of publishing a journal.

Arthur's nobility was transparent. He approached life with the utmost simplicity and was an extraordinarily hard-working man. I learned the pleasure of hard work by his example. In addition to writing editorials and articles for *The Mountain Path*, he edited the entire journal, often rewriting articles, reviewing books, and answering the spiritual questions of seekers. Whenever I handed him a newly printed issue of the journal, he would always give me in return the manuscript for the next issue, which he had personally typed.

If I merely say that Arthur Osborne's writings are lucid and potent, I will be doing an injustice to his stature and genius. Through his writings, he succeeds in taking the reader along with him into the realm of spiritual experience. Filled with his razor-like rational presentation and great devotion, every article is a welcome blend of *Jnana* (wisdom) and *Bhakti* (devotion).

Arthur Osborne knew the futility of gaining name and fame; hence, he never attached importance to it. He did, however, want his editorials and articles to be published in book form. He was confident that his writings would give a positive direction to the spiritual aspirations of seekers of all religions and backgrounds. He specifically expressed this to me.

I am happy that InnerDirections Publishing has fulfilled this cherished wish of Arthur Osborne. In doing so, it renders a unique service.

V. Ganesan
Former Managing Editor
The Mountain Path

Preface

While we were living in a cottage in India, at the ashram of Sri Ramana Maharshi, rainy monsoon days gave my wife and me the opportunity to reread back issues of *The Mountain Path*, the journal founded and edited by Arthur Osborne. In reviewing Arthur's writings, we were struck by the breadth of subject matter and the depth of insight he brought to each article. He was more than just a gifted writer; his words reflected a deep understanding of subtle spiritual matters. Some years later, after returning to the United States, we began the process of selecting Arthur's editorials for eventual publication.

Because of the depth of his own experience, Arthur would completely immerse himself in the subject he was exploring. His unique insights cover the many facets of the spiritual life. Each article offers a distinct perspective that is always refreshingly original and clearly presented.

While we have edited the articles in *For Those with Little Dust* to reflect a more contemporary use of language, we have left their meanings unchanged. Only a few of the articles in this edition have come from sources other than *The Mountain Path*, which were published by Sri Ramanasramam in the small book, *Ramana Arunachala*. We included them to broaden the understanding of Ramana Maharshi's humanity. Additionally, we added a few of Arthur's poems throughout the book; he had a great love for poetry, especially poems that reflect higher truth.

Arthur uses three terms repeatedly throughout the book that come directly from Ramana Maharshi's teachings: "Self," "Self-inquiry," and "Heart."

Sri Ramana used the term "Self" when describing the ultimate reality. After all, what could be nearer and more intimate than one's own Self? In whatever language we refer to ourselves as a person, we always say "I" or "myself." Normally, this "self" is perceived through the filter of the ego—the imposter "I" that provides a limited understanding of who and what we truly are. However, when we realize our original nature, we still refer to ourselves as "I" or "myself," but the self we refer to is no longer limited to the body/mind organism. It is the supreme "Self"—the infinite Being, which is called by many names: God, Supreme Being, Consciousness, Reality, *Nirvana*, etc.

"Self-inquiry" is also a term used throughout the book. It specifically refers to the "method" that Ramana Maharshi taught for realizing our eternal, joyous nature. Self-inquiry involves going to the root of all self-misunderstanding—the "I-thought." Regardless of the method one adopts to seek Liberation, whether through a system or nonsystem, there still exists an effort-maker—the "individual." Maharshi repeatedly asks us to discover the nonexistence of this individual through use of the *vichara* (the inquiry "Who am I?"). In essence, we trace the "I-sense" back to its source and remain there.

As the presence of the underlying Reality begins to dawn within, we recognize the enormous limitation in identifying with the personal "I," and the sense of being a "separate individual" begins to dissipate. Subsequently, the Universal "I" or Pure Awareness (which is always available) reveals itself as our true Self. Maharshi expresses this wonderful realization in the following manner:

> The "I" casts off the illusion of "I" and yet remains as "I." Such is the paradox of Self-realization.

The third term that Sri Ramana often uses is "Heart." This refers to the spiritual center of consciousness rather than the physical organ. As we begin to abide in the Heart, the mind becomes free from its latent tendencies. Although the practice requires effort in the beginning, it is, by nature, effortless, for it is our natural state of Being.

These three terms, which Arthur refers to frequently throughout the book, drive home the clarity and radical simplicity of Maharshi's teachings.

We are grateful for the kind support of Sri Ramanasramam,

with whose encouragement these selections have been published. We hope that Arthur's writings find a place in the heart of spiritual aspirants everywhere, regardless of their background or tradition. Oneness of Being knows no time or limitation; these articles, though written more than thirty years ago, still maintain their deep significance.

Matthew Greenblatt
Carlsbad, California

The Cosmic Dance

Things flow as they will flow.
Your Self the screen on which is cast
The shadow land;
Your Self the void wherein flows past
The rhythmic band.
In Consciousness all is; all things join hand
In cosmic dance;
All circumstance,
Past and to come, weaving an endless strand,
Is now.
Things flow as they will flow.

Arthur Osborne

Part I

Osborne's Quest

Introduction

By Lucia Osborne

Arthur Osborne was born in London on September 25, 1906. His father was a school headmaster, while his mother was a simple gentlewoman as loveable as she was impractical. From her, Arthur must have inherited his bent for poetry, for she spent much of her time writing poems amidst her flowers.

When still a schoolboy, Arthur wanted to become a farmer and spent a lot of his free time in their garden, helping his father. However, his father had other plans for him, particularly after he won an exhibition in English literature that was open to schoolboys throughout England. So he took his degree in history at Oxford, where he could have stayed on as a don, and later, professor. However, he rejected this career because he was seeking a meaning and purpose to life, and he realized that research into particular periods in history would not provide the answer he was seeking. As he expressed later, he rejected both consciously and instinctually a life lived without meaning. Perhaps in one who does not even know that there is anything to seek for, rejection serves as a beginning of the search.

After leaving Oxford and traveling for a while in Italy and other places, Arthur went to Poland, where we met and later married. He spent four years in Poland, the greater part of them teaching at a maritime college and acting as secretary to the Anglo-Polish Society. He managed its affairs with his usual efficiency, even writing plays for their entertainment that used to bring the house down because they were so funny.

A friend introduced him to René Guenon's early books, which emphasized that Being is One, and by realizing this, one's true identity is realized. The impact of Guenon on Arthur was tremendous. His restlessness and discontent fell away with the realization that life had a meaning after all. When he read the sentence that "Being is One," he felt immediately that it was true and that he had always known it, though not consciously. He also recognized that if Being is One, and there is no "other," then "who am I?" The "I" cannot be other than the One Being. Therefore, to realize one's true Self is to realize one's Identity with the absolute One Being.

This realization marked the beginning of the quest from which he was never to turn back. Arthur soon realized that all religions teach about our supreme identity—Eastern religions openly, and Western ones often veiled behind esoteric terminology. Esoterically, then, religions are unanimous, diverging only in their external application, ritual, social organization, and code of conduct.

A group, which had gathered around Guenon, followed a guru Guenon approved of. Members of the group urged us to join them and receive initiation, which we did when Arthur got a job as lecturer at the Chulalongkorn University in Bangkok. There we both followed a rigorous *sadhana* based largely on ritual, prayers, and invocation. The discipline helped us prepare for inner growth, especially since we did not fit into the social life of Bangkok and were content to lead a life withdrawn from its busy activities. Our spiritual practices took a good deal of our time in any case. I later learned that Arthur's students at the university shared the consensus that he was the wisest teacher they ever had. They called themselves "Osbornians."

We heard about Ramana Maharshi for the first time while in Poland. One member of our group was in India, living at his Ashram. This news created a curious feeling of nostalgia within us. Later, in Bangkok, Arthur received two of Maharshi's booklets, *Who Am I?* and *Upadesa Saram* (*The Essence of Instruction*). The photograph of Ramana Maharshi in one of the booklets was so impressive that it strengthened our resolve to go to India and see him. After three years at the University, Arthur got six months' leave and two friends from the group arranged for us to go first to Kashmir; it would have been far too hot in Tiruvannamalai at the time for our three small children. The eldest, Kitty, was not yet five; Adam was about three; and Frania was six or seven months old. It was the beginning of the hot season, so we stayed in that beautiful valley with our friends for several months, continuing our spiritual practices as before. In September, Arthur went back to Bangkok alone. World War II was drawing nearer to Siam, and women and children were advised not to remain there. So, at last, I left with the children to Tiruvannamalai, where our friend had kindly put his house at our disposal. We were going to live near the sacred hill Arunachala and the abode of Ramana Maharshi! As for Arthur, a little while after his return to Bangkok, the Japanese invaded Siam, and all the Westerners were interned for the duration of the war. We had no news at all of each other until his release four years later.

During internment, Arthur continued pursuing his spiritual practices, which made him rather conspicuous in such a confined place. Several people became interested and asked questions, and Arthur's replies so convinced them of higher truth that one of them later came to Tiruvannamalai and became a devotee of Ramana Maharshi. Characteristically enough, Arthur made a flower garden in the camp that was occasionally rocked by bombs. Throughout his internment, Arthur strongly felt Ramana Maharshi's support and grace. How strange that he should have turned to Sri Bhagavan and felt his grace while pursuing the initiatic practices given by a Western guru.

When the Japanese surrendered, Arthur left for Tiruvannamalai. He arrived with the preconceived idea imparted to him by the above mentioned group that Ramana Maharshi was not a guru; that, great as he was, he did not give initiation; and that he had no disciples.

Sri Bhagavan did not immediately reveal himself to Arthur.

In fact, the first impression of Maharshi was less striking than his photographs had made him seem. The change came a few weeks later during a festival for which huge crowds came to Tiruvannamalai and the Ashram. The people were sitting in the courtyard in front of Sri Bhagavan, with Arthur in the front row. Arthur describes what happened to him in his autobiography:

> He sat up facing me, and his luminous eyes pierced into me, penetrating, intimate with an intensity which I cannot describe . . . then quietness, a depth of peace, an indescribable lightness and happiness.

This initiation by look vitalized him and he began to practice Self-inquiry, which as a *sadhana* suited his temperament perfectly. As Arthur's practice deepened, the *vichara*, the constant inquiry began to awaken an awareness of the Self as Bhagavan outwardly and simultaneously as the Self within. The erroneous theory that Bhagavan was not a guru had simply evaporated in the radiance of his grace. He now perceived that Bhagavan's teachings were extremely practical, offering people specific guidance in their *sadhana*, according to their aptitude.

Arthur found that he could no longer continue the practices into which he had been previously initiated. He forced himself to continue them for some time out of a sense of duty and then asked Sri Bhagavan's permission to drop them. Sri Bhagavan agreed immediately, saying, "Yes, all other methods only lead up to Self-inquiry." Arthur then wrote a letter to the teacher in Europe that contained a definite statement that Ramana Maharshi was a guru who gave initiation and guidance. He showed the letter to Sri Bhagavan, who read it carefully, handed it back, and said in English, "Yes, send it." This was quite exceptional, since his usual practice was to hand letters back without saying anything or occasionally giving a brief nod.

Until this point, Arthur still considered going back to the Chulalongkorn University, but Sri Bhagavan obviously meant to keep him at Arunachala. Conditions in Siam made it unrealistic to return, and later the question did not arise anymore. Released internees were being evacuated back to England and given priority and help in readjusting their interrupted careers. Out of kindness and concern about our future, the British High Commissioner kept urging us to return to England; finally, he wrote that the last boat was leaving on a specific date. We did not even show these letters to Bhagavan. It was impossible to consider leaving him and living somewhere else. From a worldly point of view our decision was very unpractical, a sort of divine madness. We had three children to be educated and no adequate prospects in Tiruvannamalai for a man with Arthur's qualifications. In fact, he did have a hard time of it later when work became necessary away from the Ashram. First, he took a job on a newspaper (as if in preparation for his work on *The Mountain Path)* and later spent four years as the principal of a school. With his usual efficiency and thoroughness, he did these jobs successfully, but conditions were far from congenial. He spent holidays and any free days from work in Tiruvannamalai.

After Bhagavan's *Mahanirvana* (death), Arthur wrote a number of articles about him for various newspapers. He collected these together and, after editing the articles, he gave them to the Ashram to publish as *Ramana-Arunachala*. The second book he wrote was *Ramana Maharshi and the Path of*

Self-Knowledge. Later, he wrote *The Incredible Sai Baba* and *The Rhythm of History*. The next book was *Buddhism and Christianity in the Light of Hinduism*, followed by *The Collected Works of Ramana Maharshi* and *The Teachings of Ramana Maharshi in His Own Words*. While in Calcutta, Arthur also wrote a book for young people, entitled *Gautama the Buddha,* with a foreword by the Dalai Lama. At that time, he also wrote *The Question of Progress,* which was a series of lectures given in Madras to university professors. These books, particularly about Ramana Maharshi, have been instrumental in spreading Maharshi's teachings throughout the world. Toward the end of his life, Arthur received many letters thanking him for having written them. His lucid, simple though erudite expositions, written from genuine understanding, with himself always in the background, served as important pointers for many people who viewed his work as a turning point in their spiritual life.

After spending four years in Calcutta as a school principal, events took a turn that allowed us to retire to Tiruvannamalai to a simple life of *sadhana*. Before we left Calcutta, a group of boys and teachers came to see Arthur and bid him goodbye, many actually weeping.

Arthur started *The Mountain Path* magazine in 1964, along with V. Ganesan, who became the Managing Editor. Everyone agreed that Arthur was the ideal person to take this work up, and he did so with remarkable success. The magazine really became an instrument for disseminating the wisdom of the world's spiritual traditions, as testified to by their seers, while clarifying the paths available to seekers in modern times. Above all, *The Mountain Path* spread Ramana Maharshi's teaching and message throughout the world. Within the short span of six years, it achieved an international reputation. Arthur single-handedly did the editorial job of several people, often writing articles under various pseudonyms if the contributions were not suitable.

In a letter that I wrote to readers of *The Mountain Path*, I described how Arthur had already prepared me for his death towards the end of 1967, even though he was in good health. He told me that he would die of heart trouble. Until then, he had never experienced any heart trouble, nor did he toward the end of his life. Yet, it was his heart that gave out in the end. Immediately after this warning, he set to work preparing complete issues of *The Mountain Path* for an entire year, finishing a number of editorials in a remarkably short time, while badly overworking. Then, his health collapsed for the first time. Within a week or so he recovered and told the Managing Editor that he had been saved this time for *The Mountain Path*. Arthur's face was so full of peace and serenity that, as Ganesan told me much later, he was under the strong impression of being in the presence of a realized person. A few months later the second collapse came, from which he never fully recovered. During our final visit to Europe, Arthur was at the point of death several times. Yet, he came through it all and I hoped that he would be with us until the end of the next year (1971), since his life followed the rhythm of four-year cycles, one of which was coming to an end. I even hoped that he would fully recover, but it was not to be. Looking through his reminiscences, I found a page towards the end, which I had not read before because it was crossed out. It is revealing:

In order to safeguard against any trace of hesitance, I

> began to practice dying—that is, being in readiness to lay down life or the mind completely. There must be no stipulation that perception of a body and the world should be restored again after dying, because that would be bargaining, not surrender. If they are restored, all right; if not, all right . . . Also, the readiness to die must not be because life is sour, oppressive, or futile. That (the suicide's attitude) carries with it the obverse that if conditions were changed and made attractive one would cling to life. That is not surrender but rebellious rejection of the terms of life offered. I had the feeling: "I am ready to give up my life but it is not accepted . . ."

St. John of the Cross writes that there comes a time in the life of spiritual seekers when activity is taken away so that they can go wholly inward. In *The Mystical Theology*, he writes: In the exercise of mystical contemplation leave behind the senses and the activities of the intellect . . . that thou mayest arise as far as thou mayest, by unknowing towards union with Him who transcends all being and all knowledge.

This state of contemplation evidently awoke in Arthur's last two years. He prepared so much material for *The Mountain Path* in advance that, relieved of all concern about it, he could devote himself wholeheartedly to contemplation.

On May 8, 1973, Arthur left this earthly scene. His death, peaceful and serene, was like a ripe fruit falling off a tree. The intervals between his breathing became longer without any sign of struggle right up to the last breath. Shortly before his death, when I was bending over his feet, I heard him say so clearly and distinctly, "Thank you."

After Sri Bhagavan's death, I thought we would be desolate, but instead of grief, we felt peaceful and often elated. He was everywhere and most of all in our hearts—the awakened living inner guru. Of course, we also experienced challenging moments, but we had the living, consoling presence of Arunachala-Ramana, guiding us through the maze of illusion and ignorance. And what about the present? People experience both life's serene and difficult moments. All that we have to do is to forget ourselves and turn to the Heart where there is no separation. As Sri Bhagavan said, "I am not going anywhere; where can I go? I am here."

The Quest and the Goal

Shortly before the Second World War, some friends sent me pictures of Ramana Maharshi and copies of some of his books. Under the influence of French writer René Guenon, who was reinterpreting forgotten spiritual traditions to the West, I had already understood that all beings manifest the one Self or pure Being, and that in essence I am identical with the Self. This means that it is possible to realize this Supreme Identity and become One with it and that the purpose of life is to do so. Until this is achieved, the illusion of separate life in one form or another must continue and, with its sufferings and frustration, obscure the radiance of pure Being. I knew that this task was the great, heroic quest, the quest of the Sangrail (Holy Grail) and the Golden Fleece, and that it required constant effort on a prescribed path under the guidance of a guru. I was making efforts to find and follow such a path, but people for whom I had the utmost respect had assured me that Ramana Maharshi was not a guru and that his teaching, however sublime, did not constitute practical guidance on a path that people could follow. I was enormously impressed by the books and pictures, by the spiritual power and beauty in them, but classed them reluctantly as a luxury rather than a utility. In any case, I could not have gone to Tiruvannamalai, because I was at the time a university lecturer in Siam. Soon, however, it became possible. In 1941, I had six months' leave, which I spent in India. Yet I did not go to see Ramana; I accepted the view impressed upon me that less-aspiring effort was more practicable, less-illumined guidance, more effective.

In September, when my leave ended, the war was already drawing near to Siam, so I left my wife and three children in India and went back alone. A friend had kindly opened his house to them at Tiruvannamalai, the only place where my wife wished to be. She was more concerned with reality than I, less with theory. I went back without seeing Bhagavan.

In December, the Japanese invaded Siam and I was arrested and interned. Just before that I had received a letter saying that my eldest daughter, then aged five, and my son, three years younger, had asked Bhagavan to keep me safe through the war and that he had smiled and assented.

There followed three and one-half long years of internment until the Japanese surrender in 1945. There was ample time for *sadhana*. Increasingly, Bhagavan became the support of my strivings, though I did not yet turn to him as a guru.

As soon as the evacuation could be arranged, I went to Tiruvannamalai, arriving there at the beginning of October; and yet it was as much to rejoin my family as to see Bhagavan that I went. Perhaps it would be more true to say that I simply felt I had to go there.

I entered the Ashram hall on the morning of my arrival, before Bhagavan had returned from his daily walk on the hill. I was a little awed to find how small the hall was, and how close to him I would be sitting. I had expected something grander and less intimate. Then he entered and, to my surprise, there was no great impression, certainly far less than his photographs had made. I saw just a white-haired, very gracious man, walking a little stiffly from rheumatism and with a slight stoop.

As soon as he had eased himself onto the couch, he smiled at me and then turned to those around us and to my young son and said, "So Adam's prayer has been answered. His Daddy has come back safely." I felt his kindliness, but no more. I appreciated that it was for my sake that he had spoken English, since Adam knew Tamil.

During the weeks that followed, he was constantly gracious to me and the strain of my nerves and mind gradually relaxed, but there was still no dynamic contact. I was disappointed, as it seemed to show a lack of receptivity in me. Yet, at the same time, it confirmed the opinion I had accepted that he was not a guru and did not give guidance on any path. Bhagavan said nothing to change my view.

Not until the evening of *Karthikai* when, each year, a

beacon is lit on the summit of Arunachala (or it may have been *Deepavali*, I am not quite sure) did a revelation occur. There were huge crowds for the festival. I was sitting in the courtyard outside the Old Hall in front of the couch where Bhagavan was reclining. He sat up, facing me, and his narrowed eyes pierced into me, penetrating, intimate, with an intensity I cannot describe. It was as though they said, "You have been told; why have you not realized?" Then came quietness, a depth of peace, an indescribable lightness, and happiness.

From then on, love for Bhagavan began to grow in my heart, and I felt his power and beauty. Next morning, for the first time, sitting before him in the hall, I tried to follow his teaching by using *vichara*, "Who am I?" I thought it was I who had decided. I did realize at first that it was the initiation by look that had vitalized me and changed my attitude of mind. Indeed, I had heard only vaguely of this initiation and paid little heed to what I had heard. Only later did I learn that other devotees also had had such an experience and, that with them, also, it had marked the beginning of active *sadhana* under Bhagavan's guidance.

My love and devotion to Bhagavan deepened. I went about with a lilt of happiness in my heart, feeling the blessing and mystery of the guru, repeating like a song of love that he was the Guru, the link between heaven and earth, between God and me, between the formless Being and my heart. I became aware of the enormous grace of his presence. Even outwardly he was gracious to me, smiling when I entered the hall, signaling to me to sit where he could watch me in meditation.

Then, one day a sudden, vivid reminder awoke in me: "The link with Formless Being? But he *is* Formless Being!" And I began to apprehend the meaning of his *Jnana* (Self-knowledge) and to understand why devotees addressed him simply as "Bhagavan," which is a word meaning the Supreme. So he began to show me what he declared in his teaching: that the outer guru serves to awaken the guru in the heart. The *vichara*, the constant "Who am I?" began to evoke an awareness of the Self as Bhagavan outwardly, while also simultaneously as the Self within.

The erroneous theory that Bhagavan was not a guru had simply evaporated in the radiance of his grace. Moreover, I now perceived that rather than his teaching not providing practical guidance, it did exclusively that. I observed that he shunned theoretical explanations and kept turning the questioner to practical considerations of *sadhana*, of the path to be followed.

It was *that* and that only that he was here to teach. I wrote and explained this to people who had misinformed me and, before sending the letter, showed it to him for his approval. He approved and handed it back, encouraging me to send it.

Daily I sat in the hall before him. I asked no questions, since the theory had long been understood. I spoke to him only very occasionally about some personal matter. Yet, the silent guidance was continuous, strong, and subtle. It may seem strange to modern minds, but the Guru taught in silence. Bhagavan was not unwilling to explain when asked; indeed, he would answer sincere questions fully. However, the real teaching was not the explanation, but the silent influence; the alchemy worked in the heart.

I strove constantly by way of *vichara*, according to his instructions. Having a strong sense of duty or obligation, I continued to use other forms of *sadhana*, which I had undertaken before coming to Bhagavan, although I now found them burdensome and unhelpful. Finally, I told Bhagavan of my predicament and asked whether I could abandon them. He assented, explaining that all other methods only lead up to *vichara*.

From the moment of my arrival at Tiruvannamalai, there had been no question of my leaving again. This was home—even at the very beginning when I was so mistaken about Bhagavan and even when material prospects seemed bleak. Perhaps that was why Bhagavan, in his graciousness, bestowed the initiation on one who sought but had not the wit to ask.

This period of constant physical proximity lasted up to the beginning of 1948. I did not think I was in a financial position to spend nearly three years at an ashram, but circumstances adapted themselves to the will of Bhagavan. Not only did his grace keep me there, but it also enabled me to go through the long period of unemployment and other trials and bereavement without undue anxiety. Although he never spoke of my difficulties or misfortunes, he flooded my heart with peace.

Early in 1948, constant physical proximity with Bhagavan had ceased to be necessary, and professional work had become urgently necessary, so I found work in Madras. I took with me a life-sized photograph of Bhagavan painted over in oils—a gift from Dr. T. N. Krishnaswamy, a devotee and photographer. I showed it to Bhagavan before leaving, and he took it in his hands and returned it, saying, "He is taking Swami with him." Since then it has looked at me with the love and compassion of a guru and has spoken more profoundly than all the other portraits.

From then on, I went to Tiruvannamalai only for weekends

and holidays, and each visit was revitalizing. I was there during one of the operations that Bhagavan suffered and had *darshan* immediately after it. The graciousness of his reception melted the heart and awoke remorse to think how great was the reward for so little effort made on my part. I was there that fateful April night during the death of his body and felt a calm beneath the grief and a wonder at the fortitude Bhagavan had implanted in his devotees to bear their loss. Gradually, one after another began to discover in the heart the truth that Bhagavan had not gone away but, as he promised, is still here.

Since that day his presence in the heart has been more vital, the outpouring of grace more abundant, and his support more powerful. The grace that emanates from the tomb is the grace of the living Ramana.

During the years he was in the body, I felt no urge to write about Bhagavan. After his death, I dreamed that he called me up to him and, as I knelt before his couch, placed his hands on my head in blessing. At this time, an impulse came to write about Bhagavan and especially to explain the accessibility of the path of Self-inquiry, which he taught.

The Indweller

He? — You? — I? — That which is,
Indwells this body, sees the living world,
And is the world it sees. Pure bliss of being,
As on a spring day, couched upon a bank.
Of grass and flowers, watching the clouds sail
by—
For a brief moment thought—and fancy-free:
But now no moment, now a well known state.

Sri Ramana Maharshi

Part II

The Direct Path

The Man Called Ramana

It was the most majestic film I have ever seen, the most awe-inspiring and yet without incident. There is a view of Arunachala hill from the Ashram drive, and then a tall, frail, light-complexioned man with short, white hair descends the slope of the hill with the aid of a staff. Then he comes out of the Ashram hall, stops to smile at a baby, walks across the grounds—just simple, everyday actions, and yet the beauty of them was breathtaking. The simplicity was so natural, the smile so spontaneous, the majesty so inherent.

His complexion was pale, almost golden, his white hair and beard always short, as the Ashram authorities gave him a shave every full-moon day in the manner of *sannyasins*. Emaciated, aged beyond his years with the burden of our sorrows, stiff-kneed with rheumatism, he leaned heavily on his staff as he walked, his eyes cast down. He had an air of modesty, utter simplicity, and childlike defenselessness. The mere sight of him walking across the Ashram ground was enough to grip the heart. People who seemed unconcerned with spiritual matters would gaze at him with love in their eyes.

The story of Bhagavan Sri Ramana Maharshi is simplicity itself. Born in a poor *Brahmin* family in South India in 1879, he went to a mission school where he learned a little English. He was a normal, healthy boy, fonder of sport than study. At the age of seventeen, when any adolescent might pass from boyhood to manhood, the great change came over him. One day a sudden, intense fear of death assailed him, a feeling of the immediate imminence of death. There was no one to turn to, no one to give help. He felt that he must face it alone. Lying in a rigid position upon his bed, he tried to visualize, to dramatize death. He held his breath to make the experience more vivid, thereby unconsciously practicing the technique of *pranayama,* or breath-control. He said,

> Well then, now death is come. What does it mean? This body is dead. It will be carried to the burning *ghat* and there burned and reduced to ashes. But with the death of this body am "I" dead? Is this body "I"?
>
> —*Self-Realization*, by B.V. Narasimha Swami

All this was no dull-thought. Vividly, the living truth flashed before him that he was neither the inert body nor the thoughts that pass and are gone. He was the eternal "I," the deathless

Spirit. In that moment, death was vanquished; he awoke into Enlightenment of the eternal Self. A lifetime of striving and *sadhana* was, for him, compressed into that brief moment. He later learned the theory of Enlightenment and recognized it, just as a woman who had borne a child might read afterward about childbirth.

His whole manner of living changed. He lost all interest in external things and would fall constantly into the bliss of the Self. After his father died, his elder brother, who was designated by his uncle to lead the family, resented the change and rebuked him one day for behaving like a *sadhu* while enjoying the benefits of family life. The young Ramana, recognizing the justice of the rebuke, secretly left home in 1896 and went to the sacred hill of Arunachala, where he remained for fifty-four years until, on April 14, 1950, he parted from the body he had worn.

For some time after his arrival at Arunachala, he remained immersed in the effulgence of bliss, barely conscious of his body, not needing it, not speaking or moving, and scarcely eating, so that to onlookers it appeared to be the most intense *tapas*.

It was not really *tapas* at all. He was simply ignoring the body that he had ceased to need. He once indicated this by saying, "I did not eat, so they said I was fasting; I did not speak, so they said I was observing *mouna*." He was already a *Jivanmukta,* a liberated being. Living in unwavering consciousness of his identity with the Self, he had no karma left to wipe out, no sin to atone for, and no further goal to attain.

For a while, he made his abode in the underground vault of the great temple at Tiruvannamalai and, immersed in *samadhi*, took no heed of the ants, mosquitoes, and vermin, though his back and thighs became an open wound from them. Some *sadhus* took him a single cup of thin gruel each day, which was all his food; finally, they carried him out bodily while he was immersed in *samadhi*.

His body was so neglected that it might not have endured long, and he might have effortlessly discarded it. So the story would have ended. However, for us the story began when compassion for those who gathered around, seeking his grace and guidance, drew him back to a full bodily life. From then on, there was a motive for continuing in bodily form—the motive of compassion. Yet, it might equally be said that there was no motive but a simple fulfillment of *prarabdha karma*, just as the sun gives life to plants and animals without purpose, simply by being itself. He compared the *prarabdha karma* of a *Jnani* to the movement of an electric fan after the current has been turned off: It continues to rotate from past momentum although no new momentum is added. Perhaps these two aspects of truth coalesce if one remembers that compassion in the *Jivanmukta* means not individual but cosmic compassion.

One of the spiritual paradoxes is that one who lays down one's life finds it; one who surrenders one's individuality becomes more individual than anyone else. The *Jivanmukta* has dissolved the ego, which exploits and perverts one's individual characteristics, and therefore these characteristics can grow to their true likeness, neither stunted nor warped, shining forth more clearly than in other people. In two masters, divine grace will be the same, but the characteristics of the human vehicle will be quite different.

Bhagavan Sri Ramana was meticulously exact, closely observant, practical, and humorous. His daily life was conducted with punctiliousness that Indians today would have to call purely Western. Everything had to be precise and orderly. The Ashram hall was swept out several times daily. The books were always in their places, and the cloths covering the couch were scrupulously clean and beautifully folded. The loincloth, which was all he wore, was gleaming white. The two clocks in the hall were adjusted daily to radio time, and the calendar was never allowed to fall behind the current date. The routine of life flowed in a regular pattern.

Bhagavan was affable and courteous to all visitors. He expressed no pontifical solemnity in his exposition. On the contrary, his speech, whether on daily affairs or on doctrine was vivacious and full of laughter. So infectious was his laughter that even those who did not know Tamil would spontaneously join in.

Right up to the end he joked, and yet his jokes also bore instruction. When the doctors were alarmed to see a new tumor pushing up during his final sickness, he said, laughing, "Why do you worry? Its nature is to come up." When a woman beat her head against a post outside his room in grief, despite his insistence that the body's death was no cause for grief, he listened for a moment and then said, "Oh, I thought somebody was trying to break a coconut." A devotee asked why his prayers were not answered, and Bhagavan replied, laughing, "If they were, you might stop praying."

His face was like the face of water, always changing and yet always the same. He would be laughing and talking, then he would turn graciously to a small child or hand a nut to a squirrel that hopped onto his couch from the window, or his radiant, wide-open eyes would shine with love upon some devotee who had just arrived or was taking leave. Then, in silence a moment later, his face would be rock-like, eternal in its grandeur.

The love that shone in his eyes, the luminous understanding, cannot be described. Someone came to the Ashram broken down with the hopeless grief of bereavement, and after hearing the story, Bhagavan simply looked, no word spoken, and peace flooded the visitor's soul.

An old pundit, who knew Sri Ramana as a boy and who had visited many yogis, decided to visit "Yogi" Ramana also and discuss philosophy with him. However, standing before the couch, the pundit felt his whole body electrified with awe, and before he knew what had happened, he fell on his face before Bhagavan. Little children were drawn to him and gladdened by his smile. A laborer picked up a blown sheet of paper, and, seeing Ramana's picture on it, he exclaimed, "Bhagavan!" and folded it reverently to take away with him. Like people, animals were drawn to him. Once he came back late from his afternoon walk on the hill, and while devotees clustered in groups or sat waiting or followed him up the hillside, a pair of monkeys came to the doorway of the hall and, forgetting their fear of people, they came inside and gazed anxiously at the vacant couch. A monkey that has been tended by humans is ostracized by its fellows on its return to wildlife, but any that had been tended by Bhagavan were gladly received. Having transcended the ego, Maharshi transcended fear and antagonism, and animals sensed this. A snake crept over his leg, and he did not move or shrink. When a devotee asked him later what it felt like to have a snake pass over one, he replied, laughing, "Cold and moist."

During the last years, the pattern of his daily life was as follows: At five o'clock in the morning, the hall in which he had been sleeping was opened, and devotees came in and sat in meditation while the *Vedas* were chanted. At six, he went to the bathroom, and at seven, there was breakfast in the Ashram dining hall. Devotees sat before him again in the hall from eight until eleven, with a break of about one-half hour at ten o'clock. Sometimes all sat silent, and the silence was vibrant with his grace. It was a peace and fullness in which words would be a distraction; at times it was an intense spiritual striving, watched and guided by him, though he might seem to take no notice of it. Sometimes someone would ask questions or sing in praise of Bhagavan. The mail arrived between nine and ten, and Bhagavan would read letters and look at newspapers without breaking the current of silence in the hearts of those whom he was guiding. He did not answer letters himself, but handed them over to the Ashram office; the replies were submitted to him for approval the same afternoon.

Lunch was at eleven, and during the last years Bhagavan consented to rest his frail body for awhile after lunch, so the hall was closed to devotees. Their loss was the squirrels' gain, for the whole floor was strewn with nuts. Devotees came to the hall again from three to nearly five when Bhagavan used to walk on the hill for about half an hour. However, during the last two years or so, he was too infirm. His knees were swollen with rheumatism, and he could only walk very slowly across the Ashram grounds. Before five-thirty in the afternoon, the chanting of the *Vedas* began again. At six-thirty, women left the Ashram and an hour later the men left.

The consideration that Bhagavan showed to people and animals extended even to inanimate objects. Every action had to be performed intentionally and nothing was wasted. I have seen the meticulous care with which a book was bound and cuttings pasted, and have heard an attendant reproved for wanting to cut into a new sheet of paper when one already started would suffice. Our exploitation of nature is ruthless today; it is more a rape than a harvesting. Therefore, it was a chastening sight to see the divine embodiment so careful in the use of things. He especially never wasted food. He might distribute a gift of fruit to children who were present or to monkeys who tried to steal it, but he never wasted anything. We mistakenly think that economy goes with frugality and generosity with extravagance, yet very often the frugal are wasteful and the generous are careful. When Bhagavan had finished a meal, the banana leaf on which he had eaten was as clean as though it had been washed. Not a grain of rice was wasted. In former years, when his body was more robust, he used to help in the kitchen, preparing meals, and he insisted that even the parings of the vegetables should be used as cattle feed and not thrown away.

Although all wished to obey him, Bhagavan's life was, notwithstanding, a lesson in submission. Owing to his refusal to express any wish or desire, the Ashram authorities built up their own structure of regulations, and Bhagavan obeyed them without hesitation. If devotees found them irksome, they had before their eyes the example of Bhagavan's own submission. If Bhagavan ever resisted it was likely to be in the interests of the devotees. Even so, he acted usually in silence and often in a manner dictated by his shrewd sense of humor. An attendant once rebuked a European woman for sitting with her legs stretched out. Bhagavan at once sat up cross-legged and continued so, despite the pain caused by the rheumatism in his knees. When the devotees protested, he replied that the attendant's orders were for everyone. Only when the lesson had been driven home did he consent to relax.

But it was not only Bhagavan's submission to regulations, but his submission to all the conditions of life, including pain and sickness, that taught us silently that pain cannot disturb the equanimity of one who abides in the Self. Throughout the long and painful sickness that finally killed his body, he submitted loyally, one after another, to the doctors who were put in charge, never complaining or asking for a change of treatment. If there was ever any inclination to try a different treatment, it was only so that those who recommended it should not be disappointed; and even then, the treatment depended on the consent of the Ashram authorities. If there is a tendency to regard submission as spiritless, it is only because we regard egoism as natural. Doubtless, it is more spirited to fight for one's desires than to submit reluctantly to their denial, but Bhagavan showed us the way to freedom from desire. Such freedom is not the submission of the dejected, but the joy of unity, for one does not submit to a stranger but to the Self.

Because Bhagavan sought to free us from psychic as well as physical desires, he disapproved of all freakishness and eccentricity and all interest in visions and desire for powers. He liked seekers to behave in a normal and sane way. For he was guiding us towards the ultimate Reality, where perceptions and powers which people call "higher" or "miraculous" are as illusory as those they call "physical." A visitor once related how his guru died and was buried, then three years later returned in tangible bodily form to give instructions. Bhagavan sat unmoved—as though he had not heard. The bell rang for lunch, and he rose to leave the hall. At the doorway he turned and quoted, "Though a man can enter ever so many bodies, does it mean that he has found his true Home?" One of the most delightful examples of his humor was when he was asked, "If somebody who desired certain powers obtained *Moksha* directly through the force of *sadhana,* would he automatically acquire the desired powers?" Bhagavan replied, "If he obtained *Moksha,* it would not harm him even if he did have power."

No one could be more simple and unostentatious. He called nothing his own and never asked for anything. He accepted the food and clothing that were necessary, but nothing more. The only outer gifts that one could make were fruit and flowers, which were taken to the dining hall and shared among all equally. Bhagavan refused to have any special consideration shown to him. If those who were sitting in the hall started to rise when he entered, he motioned to them, almost impatiently, to remain seated. I have seen him refuse to have an electric fan switched on because the devotees would not benefit equally. Afterward, ceiling fans were installed and all benefited alike. Once, when an attendant was placing a quarter mango on each person's leaf and slipped a half mango on Bhagavan's, he angrily put it back and took a small piece.

One can say "angrily" because he could show anger at misdemeanors on the part of attendants. They were small outer lapses that called for small outer disapproval. However, when it came to the failures and shortcomings of the devotees, his patience was inexhaustible. He never asked anyone to come or told any to go; he never pressed anyone to stay. Yet he watched over each one with the loving solicitude of a mother for her only child. Not that the solicitude was always outwardly manifested, however; there were cases often enough when the attention might flatter the vanity of the devotee or arouse the jealousy of others, both of which Bhagavan was shrewdly careful to avoid.

There was never any question among the devotees what mood he was in, for he had no moods. How could he, when he never for a moment mistook the form for Reality? No moods of abstraction were needed because, while fully human, he was also fully in *samadhi*, fully divine—the same when talking and when sitting silent. He merely responded according to the needs of those who approached him, and therefore all visitors felt that they enjoyed his special grace. Only the more observant perceived that every devotee enjoyed Bhagavan's special grace. Being established immutably in the Reality beyond all forms, he saw forms and events not with the inherent and graded importance that they seemed to bear for us, but by compassionately witnessing the importance that we gave them. Pundits were once sitting in the hall with Sanskrit texts, which they occasionally took up to Bhagavan to explain a particular point. A three-year-old, not to be outdone, took up his book of nursery rhymes, and Bhagavan was no less gracious and showed no less interest to him than to the others. However, the book was tattered, so he took it and supervised its mending and binding, then returned it to the child the next day, fully renovated.

Sometimes he deliberately did not recognize the importance of people's problems, for his ultimate purpose was to wean them from attachment to things and events. One of the Ashram staff died. His wife, who had been on a visit and knew nothing about it, came home in the evening, found him dead, and could not control her grief. Bhagavan said, "What is she grieving about? Nothing is changed." He said this many times during the long months when his own body was approaching death.

To all he showed unfailing courtesy. Each visitor felt at home, though often no words were spoken. If he verbally greeted a newcomer, he usually asked, "Have you been served food?" It was the first question he asked a visiting doctor a few days before his physical death, when the pain was excruciating. Yet, behind the constant equal courtesy, he individually supervised each devotee whose inner submission he had recognized. At first, one might be encouraged with the daily attention of a smile and a friendly look. Then, for weeks or months, Bhagavan might apparently ignore the person, bestowing only an occasional swift glance while the devotee sat in meditation. If a person's ego had fed on the previous attention and that person had imagined he or she was better and more favored than others, the apparent neglect might be bitter *tapas*. When wisdom and steadiness began to come, the disciple would receive an occasional smile of recognition or a deeper, fuller look from those radiant eyes of love.

It was not often that devotees spent the whole day in the Ashram hall. Many of them were householders living in the small colony of bungalows that had sprung up around the Ashram, and they had their work and housekeeping to attend to. Some could come only in the early morning and the evening. Many who lived in other towns where they had their work could come only for an occasional visit. Even the *sadhus* had to obtain and prepare their own food, for usually only visitors and newcomers were invited for meals at the Ashram.

Many desired Bhagavan to give injunctions, both for themselves and for the Ashram management, but he would not. The most he would do was to show approval or disapproval of what was done or of any project that was presented to him, and even then not always. If asked directly, he would probably keep silent or reply, "If you want to do it, do so."

Yet, his solicitous supervision did in fact cover the actions of those who had submitted to him. His approval or disapproval was usually clear enough, without being so explicit that stray visitors who had not put themselves in his hands should demand that they also be given instructions. A devotee announced his plan to leave Tiruvannamalai and take up a job with a regular salary. Bhagavan replied, laughing, "Everyone is free to make plans." The plan did not work out. An attendant admired one of the political leaders of India and wished to go to Madras to see the man when he paid a visit there. He asked permission, but the face of Bhagavan remained stone-like, without a reply. He went, rushing from meeting to meeting, each time just missing the leader or failing to gain admission. The man came back without having seen the leader, and Bhagavan teased him good-humoredly, "So you went to Madras without permission? Did you have a successful trip?" A few months after my arrival, I had business in a neighboring town and, imagining that the worldly affairs of a devotee would not interest Bhagavan, I simply asked permission to go for the day. Bhagavan gave permission but afterwards indicated that I should have explained the reasons for my going.

It might be asked why such hidden methods of guidance were necessary, why Bhagavan should not have given plain instructions. The most obvious answer is that his grace and courtesy to all visitors did not allow his making individual distinctions between them, and the devotees who had placed their lives in his hands and who thereby had acquired a right to his guidance. Perhaps he did not wish to provoke open questions as to his being a guru or indiscriminate demands for initiation, since such things were to be understood by those who went beyond words.

However, there was also a deeper, more essential answer, as the biblical statement, "By their fruit ye shall know them," affirms. One's words and actions are the fruit of one's nature. Bhagavan's silent teaching, working directly upon the heart, sought to rectify the devotee's nature and resulted in sound fruit springing from a sound tree. Control of one's actions would have been a more external method, working from effect to cause rather than from cause to effect. Bhagavan thought it best for the devotee to seek the true answer to a problem or a way out of a situation in the heart, like a schoolboy doing a sum and bringing the answer to his teacher, who would smile approvingly and give encouragement if the sum had been rightly solved. If not, the student had to work it out anew. To be told the answer would have helped the student much less.

Bhagavan found general injunctions (applicable to all), such as those religions impose on their followers, to be inappropriate. As already explained, his purpose was neither to found a new religion nor to restore the integrity of an existing one, but to open a path for all who turned to him, regardless of their religious tradition.

Towards the end, Bhagavan aged far beyond his years. He looked more like ninety than seventy. In one who had a strong constitution, who had scarcely known sickness except for the rheumatism of his last years, and who was impervious to grief, worry, anxiety, hope or regret, this would appear incredible, but it was the burden of his compassion: "He who taketh upon himself the sins of the world." Devotees came and sat before him, burdened with sorrows, tormented with doubts, darkened with impurities and, as they sat, they felt themselves carefree and lightened. How many have come and sat there, weighed down with grief, failure, or bereavement, and the light of his eyes dissolved their pain until a wave of peace flood their hearts? How many have come primed with questions, which seemed to them all-important and which their thoughts and readings had failed to solve? It might be in desperate hope or as a challenge that they brought their questions, but as they sat there the questioning mind itself experienced tranquility and the questions faded away, no longer needing to be asked. Then, if they opened their hearts, a deeper understanding was implanted there.

Even the way Ramana discarded his body was supremely compassionate. Many of the devotees believed that they could not endure or survive his physical death. When the sickness dragged on month after month, after the doctors had found it incurable and had declared that the pain must be intense (although Bhagavan did not show it), the devotees became reconciled to the inevitable. Sometimes one or another implored him to desire to be well, but in their hearts they knew that he would use no powers that they themselves could not use. Indeed, had he consented, it would have been a boon of a few years only, whereas the boon he granted was for all time and beyond time, for he said, "I am not going away. Where could I go?" Where, indeed, for he is Bhagavan. For years, his body had been tortured by rheumatism. The knees were swollen, and he walked stiff-legged and with difficulty and had to give up his daily walks on the sacred hill, Arunachala. More than a year before the end, a small tumor appeared on the left elbow. Doctors cut it out but it returned worse than before, eventually to be diagnosed as serious. Various kinds of treatment were given, and Bhagavan submitted to whatever was prescribed. Three more times it was removed, and after each operation it returned worse and higher up. By December 1949, the doctors said they could do no more. After four operations, the tumor had reached the shoulder and had gone inward. The doctors said that the pain must have been excruciating, though Bhagavan seldom gave any sign that he was suffering. The whole system was poisoned, and the last months were one long martyrdom. Yet, to the last, he insisted that all those who came to him should receive *darshan* twice a day, walking past the room where he lay. At the very end, when every touch was agony, he ordered the attendants to raise him to a sitting posture and he died sitting.

We shall not again see the divine grace in human form or the love shining in his eyes, but in our hearts he is with us and will not leave us. His grace continues to pour out, not only on those who knew the miracle of his bodily form, but also on all who turn to him in their hearts, now as before.

I have not given a clear picture of the man who was Ramana, but how can one portray the Infinite? What impressed one was his complete unself-consciousness, like that of a little child, as well as his divinity and intense humanity. We acknowledged this divinity in the act of prostration and in addressing him in the third person as "Bhagavan." To have said "you" would have been a jarring assertion of otherness. In speaking of himself, Bhagavan spoke very simply and said "I" or "this." Only occasionally, when the meaning clearly indicated it, did he use the third person, "If you remember Bhagavan, Bhagavan will remember you"; "Even if you let go of Bhagavan, Bhagavan will never let go of you."

He was unperturbed whatever happened. The majesty of his countenance was inexpressible, and yet it is no less true that he was swift and spontaneous in response and that his face was the most human, the most living, one had ever seen. He attained Realization without learning and never displayed erudition, yet he made himself better versed in the scriptures than the pundits who came to him for clarification. He was compassion itself, yet his countenance might appear immovable like stone. He was all love, yet for weeks together he might not favor a devotee with a simple look or smile. He replied to all graciously, yet many trembled and feared to speak to him. His features were not flawless, yet the most beautiful face looked trivial beside him. He often appeared scarcely to notice devotees, yet his guidance was, and still is, unremitting.

Arunachala-Ramana

There is an old saying that the sacred Arunachala hill is wish-fulfilling. I heard of it first in a remarkable way. As a newcomer, I was making my first circuit of the hill. A veteran devotee of Sri Bhagavan, who was walking beside me, said, "You must be careful not to wish for anything while on the hill or walking round it, because Arunachala is wish-fulfilling."

Anywhere else the saying would have sounded absurd. One would have laughed and said: "But surely that is just the reason why I should wish for something!" But one whose heart had opened to the spirit of Sri Bhagavan's teaching understood the admonition. When we reach a certain level of spiritual aspiration, we can justify our petitions and wishes as long as we sincerely believe them to be for the good. These include petitions for a change of fortune and mundane happiness and, better still, petitions of an unselfish nature. Like the Buddha, Bhagavan sought to free us not so much from our misfortunes, but from the wishes and desires, the fears and attachments, which make misfortunes possible. Therefore, when we come to him or to Arunachala with a wish, we deny his teaching. Bhagavan taught the path of pure *Advaita*—the highest and most serene. There was no compromise, no half measure. Since the illusory ego-self had to be denied, how could one ask for boons for it? True, those who responded to the teaching were still enmeshed in hopes and fears, still very far from having dissolved the illusion. But at least they could recognize that their hopes and fears were illusions and strive to put them aside without asking Bhagavan to indulge them.

This approach may sound demanding and Bhagavan may appear to be a hard master, but he was all love. His grace made misfortunes dwindle and took the sting from fear. In Bhagavan's presence, one felt that the magnitude of his love and serenity permeated the heart so deeply that desires and afflictions fell away, and prayers for things seemed an unworthy act. The depth of compassion in his eyes at any misfortune would heal the heart of the suffering person. At the same time, Bhagavan silently urged the person to give up attachments, to turn from the ever-frustrating ego to the ever-blissful Self. Thus, he expressed compassion not only for suffering, but even more for the ignorance that made suffering possible.

One might think that this path of pure understanding was

only for philosophers and intellectuals. However, did not simple people, both rich and poor, come to Bhagavan with prayers, petitions, and wishes to be fulfilled? In any case, they felt the silent flood of grace: peace permeated their hearts, and their attachment to whatever had caused bitterness or anxiety was transformed into love for Bhagavan. An uneducated woman said, "I don't understand the philosophy, but when he looks at me, I feel just like a child in its mother's arms."

Speaking of miracles, a businessman said proudly, "My Bhagavan doesn't give a hoot for such things." Many people who initially were not drawn to seek the Self in the heart were drawn by love to the Self manifest as Sri Ramana, who said, "Submission to God, Guru, and Self is the same and is all that is needed." They felt that Bhagavan did not wish them to ask for things. His love was so much more precious than any boon they could desire that it dissolved the petition and left them humble and openhearted before him.

According to an ancient saying, to achieve Liberation, "It is sufficient to be born at Tiruvarur, to die at Benares, or even think of Arunachala." This saying refers to the silent transmission of grace (*mouna-diksha*), for which the guru's physical presence is not needed. In this context, "to think of Arunachala" means to turn to the destroyer of desires and to renounce all petitions.

What, then, is the wish-fulfilling Arunachala, and why did Bhagavan take up his mortal abode there and compose hymns to it? From ancient times, Arunachala has been regarded as *Shiva* manifested. Arunachala is also the center of the most pure and quintessential doctrine of *Advaita*, and the path of Self-inquiry, which is the most direct path of all. *Arunachala-*

Shiva is the destroyer of "otherness" in the fire of union. Bhagavan sang in his great hymn, *Arunachala Aksharamanamalai* (*Garland of Letters to Arunachala*):

> Unite with me to destroy the duality of you and me and bless me with the state of ever-vibrant joy.

In ancient times, *Shiva* took the form of Dakshinamurthi, a Self-realized youth who taught his elderly disciples in silence. Dakshinamurthi's method of instruction suggests that the truth of *Advaita* must be realized in the silence of the Heart. Just as the doctrine requires no complicated theoretical explanations, so the path based upon it requires no elaboration of technique.

Legend has it that, throughout the ages, Dakshinamurthi has been sitting beneath a huge Banyan tree on the north slope of Arunachala in a spot inaccessible to climbers, silently imparting spiritual instruction that brings realization to any who approaches him. Until recently, however, the Direct Path of Self-inquiry has been inaccessible to humanity. Spiritual seekers neglected Arunachala, considering it less important than other spiritual centers that offered nondirect approaches that people deemed more practicable.

Bhagavan declared that Arunachala is the spiritual center of the world, because the path it represents has again become the central mode of human aspiration. For this reason, he approved keeping his Ashram open as a spiritual center after he left the body, thus making this approach available to everyone.

Some people may suppose that Bhagavan chose Arunachala for his abode because it is the traditional center of the Direct Path he taught. Such a view, however, calls for altogether too much conscious deliberation on his part. Since it was not a rational but a spiritual choice, it would be more correct to say that Arunachala chose Ramana. Even in childhood, the name fascinated him. When, as a schoolboy, he met a traveler from Tiruvannamalai and learned about Arunachala, he felt a shock and a premonition of joy that the sacred hill could actually be visited on earth. While still a youth of seventeen, he left home as a *sadhu* after Self-realization and went in search of his father, Arunachala. When he arrived at the great temple of Tiruvannamalai and stood before the inner shrine of Arunachala, the Peace which he was living became more pronounced. For the next fifty years of his life, he never again left Tiruvannamalai, the town, or the Arunachala hill.

While he was still a youth living in a cave on the hill, some devotees asked him for a devotional hymn to help them in their *sadhana*. He walked around the hill with them and, as he walked, he composed the supreme hymn *Arunachala Aksharamanamalai*, with tears streaming from his eyes as he sang it. Many years later, on that last evening, as he lay dying, a group of devotees sat outside the little room, singing *Arunachala Aksharamanamalai*. He heard it just before breath left the body and two tears of bliss trickled down from the outer corners of his eyes. At the moment of death, people saw a large star trail slowly across the sky to the peak of Arunachala as his Spirit returned to the Father. That night, while the body he had now relinquished was exposed to the view of the devotees in the great new hall of the Ashram, they spontaneously sang the Tamil verse he composed long ago, "Arunachala-Ramana."

The spiritual power of Arunachala has become active again, as it was long ago. Bhagavan said, "I am not going away; I am here." He remains here in Tiruvannamalai as before, and at the same time he is the spaceless Arunachala-Ramana, abiding in the heart of every devotee who turns to him for guidance.

The grace of Bhagavan radiates from Arunachala and from his shrine, no less now than it did while he was in the body. People are drawn there as they were to his physical presence and feel their doubts and questions melt away and their appeals dissolve in love. Often enough, the grace that pours out upon them affects their circumstances in life and includes an inner harmony reflected outwardly in their affairs, but to go to Arunachala for that purpose is to reject a great good for a lesser one. In that sense, Arunachala is wish-fulfilling, and it is better not to ask for anything.

Tradition

Streaming back, streaming back, the long hair
  of the wind!
Words spoken, songs sung, the glory-flung trail
Of the light sweeping on!
The sound of the Soundless loud-flapping the cloak
Of the ages wherein the Timeless is robed!
The echo of Silence caught by the heart
Bursting out into song!
In rhythmical measure the galaxies swirl
Round Stillness eternal in dance ever new.

The Direct Path

True spiritual masters have one purpose: to help people overcome the powerful illusion of the ego and abide in the perfect bliss of the Self. They do not expound philosophy in the academic sense, that is, to speculate upon the nature of Being. Philosophy serves only as a theoretical basis for the practical work of turning inward.

Masters use either open or veiled language in their expositions to suit the understanding of those to whom the message is given. In the East, many have declared the ultimate truth openly: only the Self *is*, that you are nothing other than the Self; that the universe is a mere manifestation of the Self, without inherent reality, existing only in the Self. We can understand this by the analogy of a dream. The whole dream-world, with all its people and events, exists only in the mind of the dreamer. Its creation or emergence takes nothing away from the dreamer, and its dissolution or reabsorption adds nothing, either. The dreamer remains the same before, during, and after. God, the conscious Dreamer of the cosmic dream, is the Self, and no person in the dream has any reality apart from the Self of which one is an expression. By discarding the illusion of otherness, you can realize that identity with the Self which always was, is, and will be, beyond the conditions of life and time. Then, since you are one-with-the-dreamer, the whole universe, including your life and all others, is your dream, and none of the events in it has more than a dream reality. You are set free from hope and desire, fear and frustration, established in the unchanging bliss of pure Being.

This explanation bears a superficial resemblance to a theory that Western philosophy once toyed with—sufficient at any rate that caution is necessary. According to the theory, only I exist and all others are figments of my mind. This would be like saying that one person in the dream creates all the others, which is absurd. In truth, the mind of the dreamer creates this person, as well as all the others.

When one realizes one's identity with the dreamer, one's own life, as well as those of others, becomes a part of his dream. Or, to change the analogy, the Western travesty has it that one character in a play is real and creates all the others, which is absurd. The truth is that both this character and the others are invented by the playwright, so that the realized one is like the actor who, knowing that the part one acts is not oneself, acts it with equanimity, unaffected by its good or evil fortune.

Generally speaking, teachers in the West and Near East have tended to veil the language of their expositions. However, no such division can be absolute. In the West, some *Advaitic* teachers have proclaimed the Supreme Identity; while in India, *Tantric*, *Dvaitic,* and *Bhakti* teachers have guided people along the paths of duality to Unity. The final goal is the same, even though those who follow the less direct paths of duality may not perceive it at the beginning, they may recognize it only in theory without making it their constant *sadhana*, or they may deny it and persecute those who proclaim it.

Some spiritual masters came to "confirm the law and the prophets" by founding a new religion. They established a complete pattern of life for a whole community, as well as a path for those who are drawn consciously towards the goal, which ultimately none can evade. Therefore, they had to clothe their more direct teaching in parables and symbols that have an outer meaning for all who do not aspire beyond a religion of ethics and devotion. In the same way, within the framework of a religion, some sought to spiritually revitalize the whole community as well as for the few who strive with consciousness of the goal. Others have confined themselves more or less exclusively to guiding aspirants on the path and have spoken a clearer language. In either case, as a genuine master, they lived and taught strictly within the framework of their religion.

Ramana Maharshi conforms to none of these categories. He came neither to found a new religion nor to give guidance strictly within an existing one, but to open a path to those who seek in all religions the world over. His teaching responds to the conditions of the world in which he came. The task performed by Sri Ramana was to reopen the Direct Path of Self-inquiry, which had become too arduous for our spiritually dark age. This path, with its theoretical basis of *Advaita*, stands, so to speak, as the source from which different religions diverge and can, therefore, be approached from any side. Whether there are many or few who take it is not the question, only that it has been made open.

Without the grace of Bhagavan, the path of Self-inquiry would probably have remained inaccessible in contemporary times, because of its very simplicity and directness. It requires no ritual or forms of worship, no priesthood or congregation, no outer signs or special observances. People can practice it in the workshop, kitchen, or city office, as well as in the monastery or hermitage.

In addition, it requires no great burden of theory. Its description as *Jnana Marga*, the path of Knowledge, sometimes leads to the idea that it is more philosophical than other paths, but the opposite is true. Like a sword, it cuts through the Gordian knot of philosophy. The structure of spiritual philosophy or science, whichever one many choose to call it, is vast; its ramifications may be bewildering. On various paths, aspirants have to master more or less theoretical knowledge—and usually the less direct the path the greater the need for theory. Only on the Direct Path does the glorious truth of *Advaita*, like a veritable sword-flash, cut through the entanglements; it is all the theory we need. The whole intricate theory of an afterlife and reincarnation falls away, since we need to discover what we are *now*, not what we will be after we die. The traditional doctrine of cycles of history is unnecessary, since, as Maharshi says, "The wise man is always in *Satya Yuga*." The complex *yogic* and *tantric* sciences of the nonphysical powers and the techniques for developing them are superfluous, since we are not all that, but the Self. Vast theories of spiritual cosmology—leading through the stages of devolution from the formless substratum down to the state of physical humanity, and the stage of one's return to the source—do not arise when we view the cosmos simply as a dream from which to awaken. Bhagavan usually refused to answer questions concerning these branches of spiritual science, repeating that we need only to concentrate on the Self that we really are.

However, Bhagavan's path is not only the most direct because of its simplicity of application and its freedom from the inessential; it is so intrinsically. Perhaps this can best be explained by outlining briefly the aspirants' initial position, the tasks before them, and finally the methods of accomplishing this.

The initial position is that *Atma*, the Self or Spirit, alone is. It manifests in all the forms of the Universe and in your being, without ever ceasing from its formless, changeless state. But there also appears to be an ego, an individual self, which imagines itself a real and separate being, as though one of the persons in a dream should imagine existing apart from the mind of the dreamer. The Self is unchanging Bliss and Perfection, without birth or death, beginning or end; the ego is in unceasing turmoil, plagued by hope and fear, anxiety and regret, attachment and bereavement, and doomed to death. However, the ego also has an intuition of the Self, which it conceives of as a greater Being, infinitely good, unfathomably wise, boundlessly loving, and it calls this being "God."

The task is to transcend the ego-sense so that only the Self, which alone was, is, and will be, remains in consciousness, seeing all this panorama as its own manifestation. As an expression of this, Bhagavan often said laughingly, "You have only to disrealize unreality and Reality will appear." This task normally means passing from unity through duality to unity. At the beginning, it appears to the aspirant that the ego is the one indisputable reality; then one feels the reality of both the ego and God or Self; and in the end, the ego-sense dissolves.

The ways of undertaking this task are innumerable, but it will suffice here to divide them into three general categories: exoteric religion, indirect spiritual paths, and the Direct Path of Self-inquiry.

The way of exoteric religion progressively replaces egoism by submission to the will of God. Its four cardinal precepts are faith, love, humility, and good deeds. As far as they are complied with, these precepts effectively lead people toward Self-realization, although this is not consciously envisaged. True, the goal is not likely to be attained in a single lifetime, but in God's patience a lifetime is very little. Faith strengthens the intuitional conviction of the reality of God or the Self. Humility, its counterpart, weakens the belief in the ego and lessens the importance attached to it. Love strives to surrender the ego to God and its welfare to others. Good deeds deny egoism in practice and are both the fruit and proof of love and humility. Therefore, Bhagavan sometimes encouraged this way when speaking to those whose nature did not draw them to a more conscious *sadhana*.

When we practice indirect *sadhana,* we strengthen, purify, and harmonize the mind by various techniques, enabling it to hold to the quest of the Self, which is often conceived as Father, Mother, or Lover. Bhagavan never denied the efficacy of such methods. Once, when a woman said that Self-inquiry did not help her and asked whether she could follow some other way, he replied, "All ways are good." However, since he was opening a more direct and potent path—one more suited to the conditions of modern life, he did consistently question people following other, less direct paths. He referred to them as "the thief turned policeman, to catch the thief that is himself." The thief is the ego or mind, which usurps the reality of the Self, and by these indirect methods of *sadhana*, the mind is trained as a policeman to catch and condemn itself.

On such a path there is the danger that the thief turned policeman may acquire police powers, and then its thievish nature may reassert itself and do far more harm than it ever could before. The ego may acquire powers and perceptions beyond the physical and then persuade itself and others that it is the Self and become that most terrible scourge, a false guru, consuming others to feed its unconfessed vanity. Or, it may simply entrench itself at some high post that it imagines to be final but which, beautiful though it may be, is no more final than the physical body is. In any case, the mind must at last be extinguished in the Self, which alone exists. Bhagavan taught that it is simpler and more direct to strive to do so from the beginning by awakening awareness of the Self and yielding [the ego] before it.

This is the Direct Path as taught by Bhagavan: to forget the ego and discover the Self, not as one self discovering another, but by awakening awareness of the Self, by beginning, occasionally and imperfectly at first, but ever more constantly and powerfully, to *be* the Self. In this sense "knowing is being."

Bhagavan instructed people to ask, "Who am I?" I am not this body which changes but leaves me the same. Nor am I the thoughts that pass through the mind and go out again, leaving me the same. Ten years ago I had thoughts, emotions, aspirations, which are gone now, but I am still the same. What, then, am I?

This is far from being a mental puzzle. Bhagavan taught that while meditating, we should concentrate consciousness on the Heart—not the physical heart on the left side, but the spiritual heart on the right side of the chest. He always insisted on this supreme center of consciousness. The following is one of the more simple illustrations that he gave about the spiritual Heart:

> When a schoolboy says "It is I that did the sum" or when he asks you, "Shall I run and get the book for you?" does he point to the head that did the sum or to the legs that will carry him to get you the book? No, in both cases his finger is pointed quite naturally to the right side of the chest, thus giving innocent expression to the profound truth that the source of "I"-ness in him is there. It is an unerring intuition that makes him refer to himself, to the Heart which is the Self, in that way. The act is quite involuntary and universal; that is to say, it is the same in the case of every individual.

He insisted that it is necessary to try, not to discuss or speculate, saying:

> You should try to have rather than to locate the experience. A person need not find out where his eyes are situated in order to see. The Heart is there, always open to

> you, if you care to enter it, always supporting all your movements even when you are unaware.

After some practice, this meditation awakens a current of awareness, a consciousness of "I" in the Heart—not the ego-sense, but a feeling of the essential "I" who is the Universal Self, unaffected by good or ill fortune or by sickness or health. We should develop this consciousness by constant effort until it becomes increasingly frequent and finally a constant undercurrent to all the actions of life. Then, if we can stop our egoism from interfering, this awareness may deepen into an ever-vaster peace beyond all understanding, until the moment when it consumes the ego and remains as the abiding realization of Self.

If various thoughts come up during meditation, one should not get caught up by them and follow them, but look at them objectively and inquire, "Where did this thought come from, and why, and to whom?" As they pass away like clouds across a clear sky, each thought leads back to the basic "I"-thought: "Who am I?" The very essence of the meditation requires that there is no mental or verbal answer. There cannot be, since the Self transcends thought and words. The ego is seeking what is before its origin and beyond its source, and the answer will not be grasped by it but will grasp and devour it.

> I came to devour Thee but Thou has devoured me; now there is peace, Arunachala.
>
> —*Arunachala Aksharamanamalai* (v. 8), by Sri Ramana Maharshi.

The beginning of the answer involves awakening a current

of awareness, a sense of Being, in the heart. This awareness is neither physical nor mental, though body and mind are both aware of it. We can no more describe it than we can describe hearing to a deaf person.

If impure thoughts arise during meditation, we should look at them and dispel them in the same way, this way base tendencies are accordingly recognized and dissipated. As Bhagavan has said:

> All kinds of thoughts arise in meditation. That is only right, for what lies hidden in you is brought out. Unless it rises up, how can it be destroyed?

Just as Self-inquiry is not a mental exercise, so also it is not a mantra. When questioned, Bhagavan replied quite definitely that it should not be repeated as a mantra, but used in the manner described.

Every spiritual path requires both purity of living and intensity of spiritual effort, and the *vichara* given by Bhagavan serves as a technique of pure and dispassionate living no less than as a technique of meditation. If anything happens to offend or flatter you, ask, "Who is injured, who is pleased or angry, who am I?" Therefore, by use of *vichara*, the "I-am-the-doer illusion" can be destroyed and one can take part in everyday life aloofly, without vanity or attachment. Bhagavan represented it as the bank cashier who handles enormous sums of money unemotionally and yet quite efficiently, knowing that it is not his money.

In the same impersonal way, we can attend to all the affairs of life, knowing that the real Self is unaffected by them; and every attack of greed, anger, or desire can be dispelled by *vichara*. It must be dispelled, because it is no use repeating that one is the Self and acting as though one were the ego. Real, even partial, awareness of the Self weakens egoism. Egoism, whether expressed as vanity, greed, or desire, proves that recognition of the Self is merely mental.

In adapting an ancient path to modern conditions, Bhagavan in effect created a new path. The ancient path of Self-Inquiry was pure *Jnana Marga*, to be followed by the recluse in silence and solitude, withdrawn from the outer world. Bhagavan made it a path to be followed invisibly in the world, in the conditions of modern life.

He never encouraged anyone to give up life in the world. He explained that such a giving up would only exchange the thought "I am a householder" for the thought "I am a *sannyasin*," whereas what is necessary is to reject the thought "I am the doer" completely and remember only "I-am." This approach can be done by means of *vichara*, equally while in the city or in the forest. Only inwardly can a person leave the world by leaving the ego-sense; only inwardly can one withdraw into solitude by abiding in the universal solitude of the Heart. This represents true solitude because there are no others, however many forms the Self may assume. Life in the world is not merely permissible, but a useful part of the *Karma Marga* inherent in the way of Bhagavan.

The outer discipline of Self-inquiry requires a constant check on actions and on the motive from which they spring. Sincerely and constantly applied, it removes the need for any formal code of conduct, for it strikes directly at egoism in every action and reaction. The impulses of the ego will not change immediately. An insult will still cause anger and a flattering remark, pleasure. Attachment to property and comfort will still continue and the senses will still clamor, but all such impulses will be exposed for what they are, so that one is able to recognize egoism and feel shame and reluctance over each of its manifestations. From that point the eradication of egoism will begin, a task demanding constant effort and remembering.

Yet, how can such a path be integral if it does not leave room for *bhakti*, that is, for love and devotion? The path of *bhakti* presupposes a conception of duality of the "other," to whom one surrenders. However, the grace of Bhagavan was too vast to exclude any possibility. Although he spoke of it less frequently, the path he opened also included surrender and devotion. He said, "There are two ways: either ask yourself 'Who am I?' or surrender." And, even more explicitly, he said, "Submit to me and I will strike down the mind."

He was not referring to another alternative path; devotion to the guru is a powerful and essential ingredient of the Direct Path that Bhagavan taught. He reminded us that the real guru is in the heart, and once the mind turns to seek the guru within, this same guru draws it ever more powerfully to himself, ultimately revealing himself to be one's true Being. But to begin the process, one needs the outer guru, for, as Maharshi said:

> The outer Guru gives the mind a push inward and the inner Guru pulls it to the center.

Bhagavan is the universal *Sadguru* who, through his grace, opens the path to everyone who turns to him; and ultimately the two gurus are One. Subsequently, it is more obviously so now than ever, since the apparent duality of outer and inner guru has been removed.

All we need is surrender. Bhagavan said, "Only keep quiet and Bhagavan will do the rest." That is the great task, through devotion to Bhagavan and Self-inquiry, to keep the mind quiet, for it is like a monkey in constant vain agitation. Only when it submits and is quiet can the guru, who is the Self, be heard.

As on every path, progress is gradual and requires constant effort, whether or not the radiant foreglow of Truth comes and goes. Bhagavan expressly warned the disciple for whom he wrote *Self-Enquiry*:

> However, the Self-oblivious ego, even when once made aware of the Self, does not get Liberation—that is Self-realization—due to the obstruction of accumulated mental tendencies; and it frequently confuses the body with the Self. Long, cultivated tendencies are to be eradicated only by long, continued meditation.

A phenomenon such as Bhagavan's own immediate realization of the Self is extremely rare, and he never led others to expect that it would happen to them. Actually, to desire success or even to think about it is itself an impediment, since it means desiring achievement for the ego instead of trying to eliminate the ego through the inquiry, "Who am I?"

The vibrant awareness of the Self becomes more frequent and uninterrupted until it awakens the moment one sits in meditation. In time it becomes constant, not only in hours of meditation, but underlying all the actions of life. In proportion, as awareness of the Self becomes stronger and more continuous, the ego grows weaker and subsequently purified in preparation for its final immolation. Bhagavan said:

> The moment the ego-self tries to know itself, it changes in

character; it begins to partake less and less of the body, in which it is absorbed, and more and more of pure consciousness, the Self or *Atman*.

The *Forty Verses on Reality,* composed by Bhagavan, is the doctrine of the Direct Path. In verses 29 and 30, he thus succinctly describes it:

> The path of Knowledge is only to dive inward with the mind, not uttering the word "I," and to question whence, as "I," it rises. To meditate "This is not I" or "That I am" may be an aid, but how can it form the inquiry?
>
> When the mind, inwardly inquiring "Who am I?" attains the Heart, something of itself manifests as "I-I," so that the individual "I" must bow in shame. Though manifesting, it is not "I" by nature but Perfection, and this is the Self.

The Direct Path awakens love through Knowledge. It is not knowledge of one by another or mind-knowledge, but the awakening bliss of the Self to which the mind is drawn and in which it is absorbed in love.

Be Still

Thou art? —I am? — Why argue? — Being is.
Keep still and be. Death will not still the mind.
Nor argument, nor hopes of after-death.
This world the battle-ground, yourself the foe
Yourself must master. Eager the mind to seek.
Yet oft astray, causing its own distress
Then crying for relief, as though some God
Barred from it jealously the Bliss it sought
But would not face.

Till in the end,
All battles fought, all earthly loves abjured,
Dawn in the East, there is no other way
But to be still. In stillness then to find
The giants all were windmills, all the strife
Self-made, unreal; even he that strove
A fancied being, as when that good knight
Woke from delirium and with a loud cry
Rendered his soul to God.

Mind, then, or soul?
Break free from subtle words. Only be still,
Lay down the mind, submit, and Being then
Is Bliss, Bliss Consciousness: and That you are.

The Two Paths

Indian spirituality lays out three paths: *Jnana Marga*, *Bhakti Marga,* and *Karma Marga*—the paths of knowledge, devotion, and action. The more technically intricate paths of Yoga and *Tantra* do not completely conform to the above three paths.

For the moment, let us consider the two great paths of Knowledge (*Jnana Marga*) and Devotion (*Bhakti Marga*). The former aims at Realization of the Supreme Identity, while the latter aims at the union of the personal self with the Supreme Self. Aspirants choose one or the other approach according to temperament. They are not in fact mutually exclusive, although they may seem to be so in theory.

> The four *Margas* (paths), *Karma*, *Bhakti*, Yoga, and *Jnana*, are not exclusive of one another. Each is, however, described separately in classical works only to convey an idea of the appropriate aspect of God to appeal readily to the aspirant according to his predisposition.
> —*The Collected Works of Ramana Maharshi*

Nevertheless, aspirants generally follow either the path of knowledge or that of devotion, often combining elements of one or the other with the path of action.

Let us start with the path of knowledge. "Knowledge" in this sense does not imply learning, theory, or philosophy, but intuitive understanding. Indeed, the indirect paths require elaborate theory. Only the bare minimum of theory is needed for the path of knowledge:

> Simply that Being is, and you are That;
> Therefore to know your essential Self
> is to know all.
> But not by gazing at, as one can know another,
> for "not two" is the Ultimate.
> Knowledge in that high sense is simple Being,
> Being alone is true.

This is the path that Ramana Maharshi teaches (although, as will appear later, he allowed for devotion, also). He called his approach Self-inquiry, the constant probing into the reality of one's Self:

- Self-inquiry leads directly to Self-realization by removing the obstacles that make you think that the Self is not already realized.

- Self-inquiry is not the same as meditation, although sometimes loosely so called. Meditation requires an object to meditate on, whereas in Self-inquiry, there is only the subject and no object. That is the difference between them.

- Concentration is not thinking of one thing. On the contrary, it excludes all thoughts, since thought obstructs the sense of one's true Being.
  —*The Teachings of Ramana Maharshi in His Own Words*

Aspirants must make the effort to suspend thought while retaining consciousness. Usually when thought ceases, one goes to sleep. What one must do is to remain awake and conscious, concentrating on the pure sense of Being that remains when thought subsides. It is not easy at first, but with effort and practice it can be done.

Who am I? "Any answer the mind can give must be wrong," Bhagavan said. In fact, the very attempt to give a verbal answer shows that the question has been wrongly considered a philosophical conundrum, when in fact it is a spiritual exercise. The answer begins to come as a current of awareness—"body-sensed, mind-known, and yet from both apart."

It is no use thinking that the mind is going to absorb or possess the new knowledge. On the contrary, it must let go and consent to be absorbed by it:

> I sought to devour thee; come now and devour me, then there will be peace, Arunachala!
> —*The Marital Garland of Letters* (v. 8), by Sri Ramana Maharshi

The devotee, or *bhakta*, on the other hand, does not go so far as to conceive of the nonexistence of the ego. Therefore, the devotee also cannot conceive of the nonexistence of the world outside the ego or the God above it. The three go together; if one of them exists, all three do.

> All religions postulate the three fundamentals: the world, the soul, and God; but it is only the one reality that manifests itself as these three. One can say, "the three are really three" only so long as the ego lasts.
> —*The Collected Works of Ramana Maharshi*

Therefore, the *bhakta*, instead of recognizing "that which is" as one's very Self, the sole survivor after the dissolution of the illusory ego or individual being, regards It as the creator and sustainer of the individual being, the God to whom the individual surrenders, the Lover whom one seeks, the Home to which one returns.

The Two Paths

Don't ask if I believe in God;
That is not the query,
But whether I believe in me,
In life and theory.

If I am then, the world is, and above
A God that made me, God whose living love
Still draws me back to Him, until I yearn
For that last ineluctable return
To Oneness with Him, otherness burnt out
In fires of love—and find out thus I am not.
As though in dream through distant lands roam.

When wake where down you lay; that too a way,
And therefore good; for every way leads home,
Though roundabout.
For those who go direct
There is an austere, high mountain path; to be
A haven to yourself, a lamp to yourself,
Knowing there is no separate you to pray
To be united with a separate God
Outside of you, knowing that there just IS.
Let scholars argue this or that is right
And follow neither; whichever way you choose
For you is right.

Christian and Muslim seekers generally take the path of devotion (indeed, the very word "Islam" means "submission"). The path of Knowledge, on the other hand, is in keeping with the original genius of Buddhism and Taoism, although both found themselves obliged later to provide devotional paths for the many who could not aspire so high. Other paths exist side by side in Hinduism. Indeed, some of the greatest saints have been *bhaktas*. Sri Ramakrishna said, "I don't want to become the honey but to remain separate so as to taste the honey." The great *Marathi* poet saint Tukaram, who spoke sometimes from the viewpoint of the Supreme Identity, was primarily a *bhakta*. He wrote, "I do not seek God-Consciousness (*Brahmajnana*). I shall always desire dual-consciousness; Thou shalt ever remain my Lord and I, Thy devotee."

In Hinduism, Buddhism, and Islam, although not in Christianity, the most widely used *bhakti* technique is invocation of the name of God. "The simplest method is chanting the Name and freeing the mind from restlessness," said Swami Ramdas, a great modern *bhakta*.

Maharshi also offered his devotees the path of devotion as an alternative to Self-inquiry. If some complained that they found this too difficult, he would often say, "There are two ways: ask yourself 'Who am I?' or surrender." Indeed, many of his devotees did, and still do, follow the path of love, surrender, and devotion. Even in this case, however, he did not give an invocation but only prescribed complete surrender to the guru. He even made the remarkable statements, "Submit to me and I will strike down the mind," and, "Only be still and I will do the rest."

It is not an easy thing to keep the mind still, without thought, or to completely surrender oneself. When one does, the barrier to Truth grows weaker and God, Self, Bhagavan does indeed break through and strike down the impostor ego. What an assurance this is to receive!

Surrender has to be complete. It includes not only surrender of all the ego's desires, but of the ego itself that has the desires, until in the end it turns out to be an illusory thing, and devotion becomes Knowledge.

Whichever path one follows, the thing is to follow it, not to argue about it. A Christian priest once told Bhagavan that he considered the goal of mystic union envisaged by Christians to be different from the Hindu goal of *Moksha* and superior to it. Bhagavan replied, "All right, attain that first and then see whether you still find any difference or anything to criticize." That was always his reply—to turn the critic from theory to practice. Argument did not interest him, only understanding and sincere effort.

Self-Inquiry

Ramana would have bequeathed us a poor gift if his guidance had been for his lifetime only. He is the Guru now as he was then. Many people who never saw him in the body find his guidance no less powerful than those who did. Therefore, no successor need give initiation in his name. The initiation was silent and formless, as it still is; the guidance went straight to the Heart, bypassing words and thought. Seekers on the path need understanding, courage, and devotion. The path is there and the guide to lead and support you to the goal.

Who is Ramana? When he joined in singing "*Ramana*

Sadguru," he pointed to his body and said, "Do you think this is Ramana?"

> In the recesses of the lotus-shaped heart of all, from *Vishnu* downward, there shines the Absolute Consciousness, which is the same as Arunachala or Ramana. When the mind melts with love of Him and reaches the inmost recess of the Heart where He dwells as the Beloved, the subtle eye of pure intellect opens and He reveals Himself as Pure Consciousness.
>
> —*The Collected Works of Ramana Maharshi*

Those who turn to the path require some method, some discipline, or some technique. Not all of Maharshi's disciples, even in his lifetime, followed the path of Self-inquiry. His grace supports his devotees on whatever path they follow, whether the focus is devotion, knowledge, or action; whether fortified by ritual or not; whether within the framework of any religion or not. Moreover, if any change becomes advisable—if any forms, techniques, or methods are outgrown and cease to be helpful—some indication will come. Guidance will not fail.

Having said this, however, the method, which Bhagavan always recommended in the first place, which he spoke of as the most simple and direct and put first in all his teaching, was Self-inquiry. It follows, therefore, that those devotees who can practice it should.

Some people have the mistaken idea that Self-inquiry is a coldly intellectual method. It is no such thing. Intellectual understanding may be helpful up to a point on one's quest, but it cannot be the quest. Discriminating "I am not this body"; "I am not these thoughts" may be a useful preliminary to the inquiry, but it does not constitute the inquiry. The inquiry is not a mental investigation such as a psychologist might embark upon. It is not a probing into the faculties, urges, memories, or tendencies of one's conscious or subconscious mind, but a quest of the pure "I"-amness that lies behind all these. It consists of turning the mind inward to the sense of Being, the feeling of "I-am."

Bhagavan gave the hint that consciousness should not be centered in the head, but in the spiritual Heart at the right side of the chest, because it is not a question of thinking but of feeling and being. This does not mean one should think about the spiritual Heart or meditate on it. When you want to see you do not think about your eyes, you just use them; so also with the Heart. It is not necessary to locate it exactly any more than locating your eyes in a mirror before you can see. It is much more important to have the experience rather than speculate about it.

A person is made up of acting, thinking, and being. Being underlies the other two because you cannot act or think unless you first are; but being is usually so covered up that it is not perceived. It can be compared to a cinema screen, with thinking and acting as pictures projected on it. The screen supports the pictures, yet is covered by them so that it is not evident. Only very rarely, for a flash, is one aware of just Being and feels it as spontaneous, causeless happiness, and pure, thought-free consciousness. The purpose of inquiry is to make one aware of Being, at will, and for longer and longer periods.

Although the term "meditation" is conventionally used for Self-inquiry, it does not fall into the dictionary definition of the term. Meditation requires an object, something to meditate on, whereas inquiry focuses only on the subject. You are not looking for anything new, anything outside yourself, but simply concentrating on Being, on your self, on the pure "I-am" of you. It is not about thinking, but about suspending thoughts while retaining consciousness.

Normally, when thought subsides, you go to sleep; and when one first begins inquiry the mind often does try to do so. An attack of overwhelming sleepiness may come over you. However, as soon as you stop the inquiry and turn to another occupation sleepiness passes, thereby proving that it was not real tiredness, but an instinctive resistance to thought-free consciousness. One simply has to be vigilant against it.

Thoughts themselves are a far more persistent obstruction. They rush into the mind in an unending stream. If you drive them out, others slip in from behind. You believe you are free from thought and before you notice it, you are indulging others. The only way out is through persistence and constant alertness. One should not get carried away by thoughts, but see them aloofly like clouds passing over a clear sky, while asking, "What is this thought? Who did it come to? To me, but who am I?" This way, you bring your mind back to the inquiry. The mind is like a monkey rushing from tree to tree, ever restless, never content to be still. It has to be checked from its restlessness and held firmly to inquiry.

However, the wandering nature of the mind and the unending succession of thoughts are not the obstruction; it is also the ego-drive behind many of the thoughts. This gives them power and makes them far harder to dispel. You may convince yourself intellectually that there is no ego and may have occasional brief glimpses of Being-Consciousness, which is unruffled happiness at the time the ego is absent. But still you are drawn to a particular person, or want to impress a special friend, or wish to dominate a specific group; you may resent criticism, feel insecure in your job, cling to your possessions, or hanker after money or power. All of these are affirmations of the ego, which you believe does not exist. So long as they exist, it does, too. If there is no ego, who feels anger, desire, resentment, or frustration?

This means that inquiry is not merely a cold investigation but a battle; every path is in every religion. The ego, or apparent ego, has to be eradicated. This is the one essential aspect common to all religions. The only difference is how to do it. Some paths will have you attack various vices individually and cultivate opposing virtues, but Self-inquiry is more direct. These progressive methods are like lopping the branches off a tree: So long as the roots and trunk remain, fresh ones will grow. Self-inquiry aims at uprooting the tree itself. If the ego is deprived of one outlet, others will develop. However, if the ego itself is dissolved, the vices in which it found expression will collapse like deflated balloons. What is required is constant vigilance until the ego is finally dissolved.

Self-inquiry, which aims at ego dissolution, does not teach one theory or doctrine. It is quite possible to know all the doctrine that is necessary before starting: "Being simply *is* and you are That." A certain amount of practice brings an increase in the frequency and length of the experience of timeless Being, which is also pure awareness and unruffled happiness. Although not based in the mind, the mind is aware of it. Although not physical, the body feels it as a vibration or a waveless calm. Once awakened, it begins to appear spontaneously, even when you are not "meditating." It exists as an undercurrent to whatever you are doing in your daily routine, whether talking or even thinking.

Concerning approach, this is an important point. It explains why Bhagavan preferred his devotees to follow the quest in their everyday lives. Sitting daily in "meditation" is useful and, in most cases, indispensable, but it is not enough. So far as possible, fixed times should be set aside for it, since the mind accustoms itself to them, just as it does to physical functions like eating and sleeping, and therefore responds more readily. For people who are bound by professional and domestic obligations, just after waking in the morning and before going to sleep at night are excellent times. But apart from that, Bhagavan would tell people to always practice inquiry, to ask themselves, "Who is doing this?"—to engage in activity without the "I-am-the-doer illusion." Keeping up this attitude of mind throughout the day's activities is equivalent to remaining alert, welcoming the sense of Being whenever it comes. Constant alertness and remembering is necessary when not formally "meditating." Initially, there will be frequent forgetting. The "current of awareness" needs to be cultivated and fostered. It is very seldom that there is accomplishment without effort.

Self-inquiry is independent of both form and doctrine. Requiring no ritual, it can be followed invisibly by the homemaker or shopkeeper no less than the monk or yogi. While the grace and support of Ramana Maharshi is available to all who turn to him, those who perceive the clarity of this path use it the most fully and the most wisely, finding an unfailing support and an inexhaustible treasure.

Predestination

The question of predestination can only be discussed from the viewpoint of ignorance, because from the viewpoint of Knowledge, there is no one to whom predestination occurs. I illustrated this point in *The Teachings of Ramana Maharshi in His Own Words*:

> It is as though a group of people who had never heard of radio were to stand around a wireless van, arguing whether the man in the van has to sing what the transmitting station tells him to or whether he can change parts of the songs. The answer is that there is no man in the van, and therefore the question does not arise. Similarly, the answer to

the question whether the ego has free will or not is that there is no ego, and therefore the question does not arise.

The problem that philosophers and theologians set for themselves is unreal, being based on the false assumption of an ego to be predestined. Additionally, the problem is insoluble, because the two alternatives are quite irreconcilable. If anything currently exists in the divine foreknowledge of an omniscient God, then it cannot be changed by free will. If this foreknowledge does not exist, then God does not know what is going to happen and is not omniscient. If life is predestined, it is like sitting in a movie theater and watching a film. We may not know what is coming next, but the ending has already been filmed according to the screenplay. However, if there is free will, it is like watching an impromptu television show in which the actors and camera operators have no idea of what will take place next.

The compromise that some theorists are fond of suggesting—that God has only predetermined important matters and left the unimportant for people to fill in—is too unintelligent and anthropomorphic to even merit refutation. In any case, who decides what is important? And on what scale of values? A young man is invited to the capital city of his country to be interviewed for a job in the Foreign Service and he decides to go. Obviously, this is an important decision since it will change his cultural and social environment, the person he marries, the children he fathers, and the whole course of his life. On his way to the airline office to book a seat on a plane, he meets a friend who invites him to travel to the capital in his car. When the young man accepts the offer, it seems like a relatively unimportant decision, which our hypothetical Grandfather God might well leave to the young man to decide for himself. However, he does not get the job, so the important decision turns out to have been unimportant. In the meanwhile, the plane he was scheduled to take to the interview crashes and all the passengers are killed.

Thus, the "unimportant decision" he made gives him thirty or forty more years of life and is vitally important not only to him but to the woman he is going to marry, the children he will father, their future wives, children, and business partners—in fact, to an unending succession of people, generation after generation. The whole theory is too absurd for discussion.

People cling to such absurdities because there is nothing a person finds more difficult than facing up to the truth of *anatta* (no-ego). Even people who accept it theoretically often find some way of avoiding its implications, perhaps because they imagine that the alternative to ego-identification would be mere nothingness.

Yet life itself proves that this is not so, since everyone experiences no-ego in the state of deep dreamless sleep and still retains a sense of existence. The only question is "who" or "what" experiences that egoless state? Actually, the alternative to the illusion of an ego is the Reality of inexhaustible, radiant Being.

So long as the appearance of an ego remains, so does the appearance of free will; in fact, they are mutually dependent. Therefore, Maharshi said:

> Free will exists together with the individuality. As long as the individuality lasts, so long is there free will. All the scriptures are based on this fact and advise directing the

> free will in the right channel.
> —*The Teachings of Ramana Maharshi in His Own Words*

In the actual affairs of life, those who have not realized *anatta* go by appearances, and it makes practically no difference whether they believe in predestination or not. In either case, they do not know what is predestined and make decisions using their initiative, and act according to their nature in doing so. Any attempt to limit their conduct on the pretext of predestination would involve the presumptuous and patently untrue corollary that they know what is predestined. For instance, suppose you are sitting on the bank of a river when a girl falls into the water. To say, “It is her destiny to drown,” and to let her drown would be a presumptuous supposition that this is her destiny. All that you know up to that moment is that it is the child’s destiny to fall into the water within reach of an adult (yourself) who is capable of rescuing her. Since what is to happen is bound up with your own decisions, it makes no practical difference whether these do not yet exist or are simply not yet known to you. In either case, the decisions are made in ignorance of the outcome.

> All the activities that the body is to go through are determined when it first comes into existence. It does not rest with you to accept or reject them. The only freedom you have is to turn your mind inward and renounce activities there.
> —*The Teachings of Ramana Maharshi in His Own Words*

Freedom to turn the mind inward implies freedom to accept or recognize one’s natural state of Realization. This invites the question so often asked, as to whether the realized person is also subject to destiny. There is a traditional saying in this connection:

> If you shoot an arrow at a running deer, and by the time the arrow reaches its mark the deer has moved away from that spot and another animal has arrived there, the arrow will pierce the other animal.

The saying implies that if a person creates karma and then becomes Realized, the karma, speeding like an arrow to its mark, will strike the Realized one, who must be considered subject to past karma, that is, to destiny. But the example is not appropriate. On realizing the true Self, one does not change into a different being but realizes that one is not a being at all, but simply *Being*. One attains freedom from identification with this or any other body/mind complex. The arrow of karma may hit the body, but one is not the body. The body is subject to karma but the pure Being of one's Self is not.

Suppose a man has a vision of a past life and sees himself as a prosperous merchant whose only son is a spendthrift who would ruin the family business if it is handed over to him. The merchant sees the situation with as much sympathy as he would when viewing a film, with no sense of personal involvement. It is not he who is wealthy, distressed, or disappointed. Even in this lifetime, an elderly man looking back may see his failures and successes, triumphs and follies of thirty years ago with an equal eye, free from emotion. Similarly, a realized person sees repercussions that could be called destiny overtaking the body that he occupies, but it does not occur to him that they concern him, and therefore he feels no emotion towards them. The body is subject to destiny, but the Self is not.

Therefore, when he was asked about destiny, Bhagavan would sometimes turn the inert question into a dynamic one by asking the questioner to find out "who" has free will or predestination, because that inquiry puts us on the trail of *anatta*:

> Find out who it is who has free will or predestination and abide in that state. Then both are transcended. That is the only purpose in discussing these questions. To whom do such questions present themselves? Discover that and be at peace.

Self-Realization as Taught by Ramana Maharshi

The experience of sages establish that Self-realization is one, whether briefly glimpsed or lived continuously as one's ultimate identity. The experience remains a glimpse only when the mind is not untainted enough to hold it. After having such a flash we must begin *sadhana* in earnest to still the mind so that thoughts and desires—the *vasanas* that make up the mind's habits and tendencies—do not veil our true nature, which is ever present.

Sri Bhagavan says that in *Nirvikalpa Samadhi,* the mind is temporarily immersed in the Self like a bucket immersed in water, but which is drawn out again by the rope of mental activity. In *Sahaja Samadhi,* the mind is merged like a drop of water in the limitless sea. The drop, which in essence is the same as the sea, has only lost its limitation, having become the sea.

The following are some of Bhagavan's statements concerning Self-realization:

- Distinctions in Realization are from the standpoint of the onlooker; in reality, however, there are no distinctions in release gained through *jnana.*
- One should inquire into one's true nature.
- The Consciousness of "I" is the subject of all our actions. Inquiring into the true nature of that Conciousness and remaining as oneself is the way to understand, through inquiry, one's true nature.
- In the Heart there shines a kind of wordless illumination of "I-I." That is, there shines of its own accord pure Consciousness, which is unlimited and one, the limited and multifarious thoughts having disappeared. If one remains quiescent without abandoning that understanding, then the egoity—the individual sense of the form "I-am-the body"—will be completely destroyed. And ultimately, the final thoughts, such as the "I-form," will also be extinguished like camphor that is burned by fire. The great sages and scriptures declare that this alone is Realization.
- Meditation on the Self, which is oneself, is the greatest of all meditations. All other meditations are included in this. Therefore, if this is gained, the others are not necessary.

Sri Bhagavan wrote with the authority of full spiritual

knowledge. Even so, he would add, “Thus say the Sages.” Like all his expositions, Self-inquiry is concerned with practical questions of the path to Self-realization. Bhagavan described other approaches, such as meditation on one’s identity with the Self and breath control, but prescribed only Self-inquiry or surrender to the guru.

Affinity with Buddhism

When Ramana Maharshi was once asked why the Buddha refused to answer questions about the afterlife, he replied, "Perhaps he was more concerned with the real work of guiding people towards Self-realization than with satisfying useless curiosity." There is a great similarity between the teaching of this modern Sage and the Buddha. Although the Buddha created a new religion destined to satisfy the needs of people far beyond India's shores, the spiritual essence remained congruent with its *Vedic* roots.

I am not referring to Buddhist cosmology which, indeed, figures much less in the teaching of the Buddha than in his later exponents. Indeed, the Buddha, like Bhagavan, preferred not to speak about theoretical concerns, since they tend to distract the questioner from the practical need for spiritual effort. The Buddha addressed the central issue of attachment to illusion, which binds people to the cycle of birth, death, and suffering. Only Enlightenment brings release. Naturally, we find this basic truth in one form or another in all religions and spiritual teaching, but it is the central theme both of the Buddha and Sri Bhagavan. Consequently, both teachers issued the direct injunction to turn away from illusion and to seek Enlightenment, rather than to follow the more indirect promise of being rewarded for virtue and punished for sin. I say "more indirect" because such teaching presents the law of Karma (the law of cause and effect) under the cloak of a moral appeal. This teaching also fastens the eyes and aspirations of its followers on intermediate states between this world and the Absolute Reality of *Moksha* or *Nirvana*. According to the ultimate truth of *Advaita*, these states, although higher and more real than the present life, are nonetheless illusory.

This refusal to prescribe any lesser goal or to recognize any contingent reality made Sri Bhagavan, like the Buddha, unwilling to speak about the afterlife. When asked, "What shall I be when I die?" he answered, "Why do you want to know what you will be when you die before you know what you are now?" That is to say, seek the ultimate truth of the Self, which alone lies behind the appearance of this or any other life. He even said explicitly:

> People do not even like to hear of this Truth, whereas they are eager to know what lies beyond, about heaven and hell and reincarnation. Because people love mystery and not

> the Truth, religions cater to them so as to eventually bring them round to the Self. Whatever be the means adopted, you must at last return to the Self, so why not abide in the Self here and now?

When seekers are preoccupied with higher, contingent states, they worship the Self as God and therefore feel separate from Him. In the ultimate Truth, however, there is no such duality. Therefore, when he was asked about God, Bhagavan replied:

> Why do you want to know what God is before you know what you are? First find out what you are. Seek the ultimate Truth of the Self, which you are.

Bhagavan also said:

> There is no God apart from the Self, for if there were he would be a Self-less God, which would be absurd.

True, Bhagavan often spoke of God, for so long as the conception of the individual self as a real and separate being continues, the conception of God as the Creator, Lover, and Judge of that being must also continue. Bhagavan spoke to each person in the idiom of that person's understanding, but to those who opened their hearts to his fullest teaching, he pronounced only the final truth: There is no God and no "you" apart from the Self.

Like the Buddha, Sri Bhagavan also refused to speak about the state of the *Jnani* (if we can call *Moksha* or *Nirvana* a state) because he refused to define the indefinable. When asked about the bodily consciousness of the *Jnani*, he would reply, "You think the *Jnani* has a body?" or "Why worry about the *Jnani* before you know what you are? First find out what you are." In this endeavor, theoretical explanations do not help and may even impede the aspirant by gratifying the mind instead of turning it toward the Self, where it ultimately merges. One of the ego's strongest defenses against spiritual effort is mental speculation. When we direct our effort to That which is beyond the mind, we should not expect the mind to ensnare higher Truth in its limited mental nets. That would be like trying to pour the ocean into a bucket. As Bhagavan said,

> The Self is self-effulgent. One need give it no mental picture, anyway. The thought that imagines is itself bondage. Because the Self is the Effulgence transcending darkness and light, one should not think of it with the mind. Such imagination will end in bondage, whereas the Self is spontaneously shining as the Absolute.

Verbally, there is a contradiction between the teaching of Sri Bhagavan and the Buddha in that Sri Bhagavan declared that there is only *Atman*, while the Buddha declared that there is no *Atman*. This contradiction lies in name only, for Sri Bhagavan used the word *Atman* to mean the Universal Self, which is *Nirvana*, whereas Buddha used it to mean the individual soul or ego. Like the Buddha, Sri Bhagavan taught that there is no individual being who endures after death—or who exists now. As Bhagavan said, "Never mind what you will be when you die; find out what you are now."

Teachers who direct their followers on a more gradual path, shielding their eyes from the blinding simplicity of ultimate Truth, have affirmed the survival of the soul after this life. However, the contradictions between the ultimate and gradual paths, like all spiritual contradictions, are only apparent. The clearest indication of this fact is that Buddhism combines the teaching of heaven and hell and reincarnation with the unreality of the individual soul. Any other life or world is as real as this one, but in truth this life also is unreal. Therefore, while spiritual effort can help us to attain a higher level of reality, we will not achieve the highest level until we extinguish the ultimate reality of the ego. Said differently, "First find out who you are."

The Buddha did not concern himself with theory. His purpose was less to construct a cosmology than to show people the way from suffering to peace. Like Sri Bhagavan, he brushed aside solutions that go only part of the way and that left only the pure affirmation of *Nirvana* and *Maya*, of the Self and illusion. And yet theorists have descended upon his teaching and elaborated complex theories that help neither themselves nor others escape from the wheel of suffering. There is a real risk of missing Buddha's real teaching, which stressed avoiding the nonessential and following the way to Self-realization. When the Buddha was asked questions within the framework of Hindu spirituality, he would sometimes answer them technically, but often he would brush them aside. He gave no ground for mental speculation and generally discouraged spiritual teachings that are concerned with the vast range of intermediate reality. Bhagavan concurs:

> Just as it is futile to examine the rubbish that has to be swept up only to be thrown away, so it is futile for him who seeks to know the Self to set to work enumerating the *tattvas* that envelop the Self, and examining them instead of casting them away. He should consider the phenomenal world, with reference to himself as merely a dream.

Not only did the Buddha not concern himself with elaborate cosmology, he cared little to establish a social order. However, he did reform social thinking mainly through the negative act of refusing to recognize caste. Whoever proved capable of following the path was capable. Sri Bhagavan had the same attitude. However, since his purpose was not to found a new religion or social order, he did and said nothing to attack caste. He simply bestowed his grace on all in the measure in which they were prepared to receive it. If the *Brahmins* chose to sit apart in the Ashram dining hall, they could—but he sat where he could view both sides. He approved of the morning and evening recitation of the *Vedas* in the hall, but no devotee, whether woman, low caste, or foreigner, was excluded from his presence during the recitation.

The difference between the teaching of the Buddha and of Sri Bhagavan primarily stems from the Buddha's founding a new religion. Therefore, he appealed to the masses as well as to seekers. Although, he stressed that Knowledge brings Liberation, he cast his teaching in a more emotional form, speaking about suffering and its relief. Nevertheless, the meaning of his teaching is clear: Attachment to an illusion causes suffering and is dispelled by Knowledge. On the other hand, since the teaching was adapted to the world at large, genuine seekers on the path, who desired its essence, had to renounce the world. Giving up home and property and entering a monastery became the outer symbol of giving up attachment and turning away from illusion to enter the Heart.

Spiritual masters bring messages needed by their cultures and their times. Most recently, Sri Ramana introduced a spiritual path that people can follow in contemporary life. It can help people who seek spiritual guidance within their own religion, but do not always find it. Since Bhagavan's teaching was directed to those who aspire to the path, he spoke clearly of ignorance rather than of suffering, and the dawning of Knowledge rather than relief from suffering. Since he was not formulating a new religion, he did ask his devotees to withdraw from contemporary life. The conditions of life make it difficult for those who crave grace and guidance to withdraw from the world or even to observe the obligations of their own religion. Indeed, Bhagavan has freed those who turn to him from the need to do so. Not only Hindus, but Buddhists, Christians, Muslims, Jews, and Parsis came to him, and he never advised anyone to change their religion. He prescribed *vichara* for all alike. So long as the observances of religion helped a devotee, Bhagavan never advised the person to discontinue them. However, when *vichara* is effectively practiced, it supersedes all other observances. In Bhagavan's words, "All other methods only lead up to *vichara*."

Bhagavan often explained that the main objective is to overcome the "I-am-the-doer illusion," and therefore it does not help to exchange the thought "I am a householder" for the thought "I am a monk." Seekers must discard both and remember only "I-am."

Bhagavan reopened the Direct Path of Self-inquiry prescribed in only slightly different form by Lao-tzu and by the Buddha:

> Self-inquiry alone can reveal the truth that neither the ego nor the mind really exists and enables one to realize the Pure, undifferentiated Being of the Self or Absolute.

Continued Presence

Days at the Ashram were filled not with an air of idleness, but with intense activity. One might compare the Ashram to a spiritual factory, with the devotees engaged in *sadhana* and Bhagavan supervising and guiding each one with meticulous, though silent, care.

All knew that they were the disciples and he was the guru. In private he spoke to them as the guru and sometimes gave instructions for their *sadhana*. In each case, *sadhana* under his guidance dated from some act or word of initiation, usually concealed. When asked whether he was a guru and gave initiation, he always avoided a direct reply. Had the reply been "no," he would most certainly have said "no." However, had he said "yes," he would immediately have been besieged by demands for initiation and forced to make a distinction between true devotees and those visitors who were not surrendered in their hearts to his guidance. His compassionate love was too great and his wisdom too shrewd to rank disciples as "higher" or "lower" than others. Indeed, he did not, since he saw the Self in all.

When asked whether he gave initiation, Bhagavan usually replied that there are three types of initiation: by speech, look, and silence. This left the burden of understanding to the inquirer. According to ancient tradition, the three types of initiation are symbolized by the bird, which needs to sit on its eggs to hatch them; by the fish, which needs only to look at them; and by the tortoise, which needs only to think of them. Initiation by silence is most natural to the *Jnana Marga,* the path of Self-inquiry.

Several formalists did indeed leave and seek initiation elsewhere, and Bhagavan said nothing to detain them. Those with understanding remained. He said to one of them, Major Chadwick, "If it had been necessary for you to seek a Guru elsewhere, you would have gone away long ago."

He was an authentic *Sadguru*, a *Jivanmukta* or perfect *Jnani*, for whom there are no others but only the Self; therefore, no relationship can be assumed. He sometimes reminded his devotees that the outer guru is simply a form taken out of consideration for the disciples' ignorance and serves to turn them inward to discover the inner guru, the Self.

In the past, spiritual masters wrote openly about theory, but have been more reserved about the practice they prescribed in case people should attempt it without proper guidance. Bhagavan, however, proclaimed the path openly in speech and writing. This accords with the silent initiation that he brought to the world. The silent initiation might descend on those who turned to him in their heart, wherever they might be. They could learn from books whatever techniques they needed. Indeed, Bhagavan sometimes reminded devotees that even the journey to Tiruvannamalai was only illusory, since the real pilgrimage has to be made in the heart.

Was the Direct Path opened by Bhagavan for his lifetime only? Bhagavan said that a guru is necessary for every seeker; he added, however, that the guru need not necessarily take human form. Only rare seekers can follow the guidance of a nonphysical guru, yet since Bhagavan achieved Self-realization without a guru's physical presence, he made this form of spiritual instruction available to devotees. His work differs from the normal mode of spiritual guidance. Throughout the ages, there have been parallel initiatic streams flowing to the Ocean of Realization, each staying within its own banks. Many have petered out in the desert or marshes, having dwindled to a mere trickle. Bhagavan has rectified this state of affairs by throwing a lifeline to all who turn to him. Additionally, if Bhagavan could forgo the usual mode of initiation and guidance during his lifetime, why not afterwards? The conditions, which called for this innovation, still exist. There are, moreover, positive indications that the guidance still exists.

When asked once whether a *Jivanmukta* continues to perform any function after physical death, Bhagavan replied that in some cases it is so.

Right up to the end, Bhagavan showed an interest in the

continued publication of the Ashram books, even revising a new edition during the last few weeks of his life. And yet the very purpose of these books was to spread the knowledge of *vichara*, the path of Self-inquiry. If that path was no longer accessible, what further need for the books would there be?

Bhagavan approved a will that was submitted to him, one of whose terms was that the Ashram should be maintained as a spiritual center when he was no longer in the body. Whatever the devotees may do, this is Bhagavan's achievement: The center is the radiation of the guru.

When his physical death was imminent and devotees complained that he was leaving them without guidance, he replied, "You attach too much importance to the body," indicating that discarding it would not put an end to their being guided by him.

In reply to a question by Dr. Masalavala, retired Medical Officer of Bhopal State, Bhagavan said, as recorded by Devaraja Mudaliar in *Day by Day with Bhagavan*:

> Guru is not the physical form, so contact will continue even after the physical form of the Guru vanishes.

Before his death, he said, "They say I am dying, but I am not going away. Where could I go? I am here." This is a simple doctrinal statement, because the *Jnani* is universal and there is no "here" or "there" for him, no coming or going, in the Here and Now of eternity. In his idiosyncratic way, Bhagavan made a doctrinal statement of universal truth, which at the same time answered the particular needs of the devotee. Though we may leave him through our lack of awareness, he cannot leave us, for he is the Self.

The Few

No argument can pierce the shuttered mind.
Let truth shine forth resplendent as the sun,
Still, crouched in their dark corner, will they find
Some guttering candle till life's day be done.
Even though we sang like angels in their ear
    They would not hear.

Those only in whose heart some inkling dwells,
Grown over though it be, crushed down, denied,
Will greet the pealing of the golden bells
And welcome truth when all around deride.
Yet sight has laid a debt upon their will
    Not all fulfil.

For even of those who see, only a few
Will have the intrepid wisdom to arise
And barter time's false values for the true,
Making their life a valiant enterprise
To vindicate their heritage long lost,
    Nor count the cost.

And out of that so noble fellowship
Questing the Grail upon the mountain peaks,
Well is it if it meet the expectant lip
Of even one persistently who seeks.
Yet is this quest the glory and the goal
    Of the awakened soul.

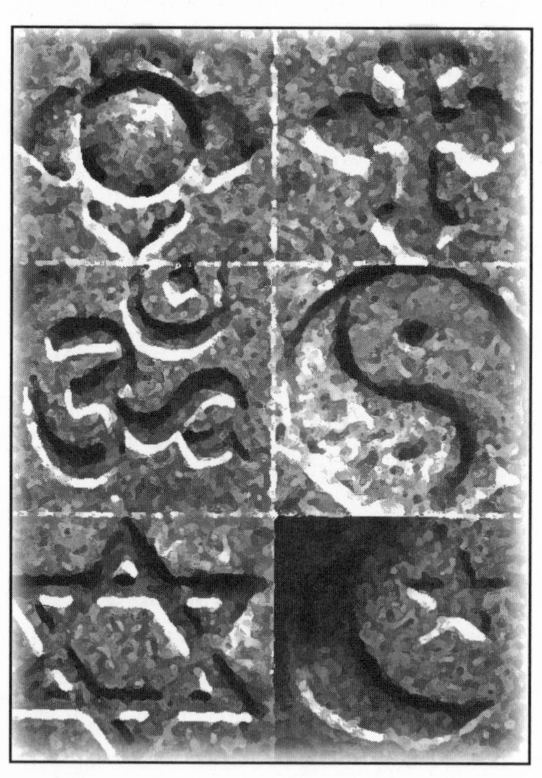

PART III

Insights on the Spiritual Quest

To Those with Little Dust

It is related (and the story is no less significant whether historically true or not) that after attaining Enlightenment the Buddha's first impulse was to abide in the effulgence of Bliss without turning back to convey the incommunicable to humankind. Then he reflected, "There are some who are clear-sighted and do not need my teachings, and some whose eyes are clouded with dust who will not heed it though given, but between these two there are also some with but little dust in their eyes, who can be helped to see; and for the sake of these I will go back among mankind and teach."

This story shows that there is a more satisfactory state than that of ignorant, confused, unguided, frustrated modern humanity, and a higher, more satisfying, and more durable alternative than any provided by wealth or luxury, art or music, or the love between man and woman. Such a state can be attained in his lifetime, and the purpose of all religions has been to lead people towards it, although in many different ways. I say "towards" rather than "to" because although the supreme state may not be attained in this lifetime, merely approaching it can bring peace of mind and a sense of well being not otherwise attainable.

Mystics often have had unsought glimpses of a higher or the highest state; those who are psychic have out-of-the-body and other experiences closed to the ordinary person; but all this means little in the quest for Realization. Such experiences may help at certain stages of certain types of paths, but they may also hinder and distract, like the sirens that Odysseus heard but against whom he made his crew plug their ears. If the pleasures of the physical world are seductive, those of the subtle world are certainly no less so. Christ said that if one attains the kingdom of heaven, all else shall be added, but that is *after* attaining. If one seeks all else beforehand, one is not likely to attain.

Those who have such powers and experiences do not find the quest to be shorter and less arduous than those who do not have them. Realization is not something like music, for which some are by nature more gifted than others. It is fundamentally different, since music requires the development of a faculty that is stronger in some and weaker in others. Realization, however, involves the discovery of and identification with one's true Self, which contains all faculties.

We cannot easily predict who can and will understand spiritual truth. It has certainly nothing in common with intellectual ability, as commonly understood. Indeed, the scriptures of the different religions agree by warning us that neither intellect nor learning is any qualification. In fact, they can generally be a hindrance:

> It is rather the unlearned who are saved than those whose ego has not yet subsided in spite of their learning.
> —*The Collected Works of Ramana Maharshi*

> The humble knowledge of oneself is a surer way to God than deep researches after science.
> —*The Imitation of Christ*, by Thomas à Kempis

A scientist may fail to understand spiritual science, a philosopher may be unreceptive to the Perennial Philosophy, while a psychologist may remain ignorant of what underlines the mind. On the other hand, a spiritual master may or may not be an intellectual: Ramana Maharshi was, but Sri Ramakrishna was an ecstatic with the mind rather of a peasant than a philosopher. St. Ignatius Loyola was temperamentally so averse to study that it required immense effort for him to gain the degree without which the Church would not allow him to teach, and he was middle-aged before he did so.

While theoretical understanding is not enough, neither is belief in the sense of a conviction that this or that will happen after death. What is needed is to set one's hand to the plough, as Christ put it, to undertake the true alchemy, transmuting the dross in one's nature to gold.

This is the quest of the Sangrail (Holy Grail), the search for the elixir of life, the eternal youth of the Spirit. It requires a willingness to open one's heart to the truth, to surrender oneself and give up the ego, and to conceive of the possibility of its nonexistence. It is the pathway of heroes, the way from trivialities to grandeur. Its consummation is like waking up from a dream into the ever-existent Reality.

Where Charity Begins

I have written that the quest for Realization is the great enterprise, the true goal of life. Yet one often hears the objection, "But isn't it more important to help others?" Although some who make this objection doubtless do so in good faith, it is essentially a hypocritical attack on spirituality. It goes back to the nineteenth-century socialists who said, "First things first. Let us first remove people's poverty, then there will be time to consider their spiritual needs." Well, they partially succeeded. There is very little poverty left in northeastern Europe. However, did Europeans then turn to spiritual support? Not at all. The anti-spiritual trend only accelerated and became more unabashed. Workers who acquired leisure, security, and competence had less time, not more, to devote to spirituality.

In fact, it is not true that welfare facilitates religion, that poverty impedes it, or that material needs are the "first things" to be attended to. Christ taught the exact opposite when the rich, young man approached him. He counseled the young man to give his property away and become a mendicant. If poverty can be an impediment, so also can prosperity. Indeed, it might well be said that in a welfare state prosperity is the opiate of the people, lulling them into a false sense of security.

One sign of the animus behind the do-good objection is that it is only used against those who turn to a spiritual path. If a person declares that his absorbing interest in life is music, business, or politics, no one will raise an objection. However, objections are raised when someone turns to religion. Why do people suppose that one who is striving to subjugate or destroy the ego is doing less to help others than one who allows it free-play? Rather, such a person is likely to do more, helping others in an unobtrusive way rather than engaging in organized charities. In general, there is likely to be less vanity and more genuine goodwill in this person's behavior.

People often apply a widely used touchstone in assessing what moral behavior is. They ask, "What would happen if everyone did that?" If everyone lived as Maharshi enjoined—in the world but not of it—fulfilling professional and family obligations with detachment, helping when called upon for help while striving on the path, there would be no need for social service, since none would be exploited or impoverished for the benefit of others. There would be no destitute to help.

This touchstone, however, has an anti-spiritual animus, being aimed, in part, against those who renounce the world to become monks or *sadhus*. It is, in fact, against those who renounce the world that the first objection mentioned—"But wouldn't it be better to help others?"—is primarily aimed, although by extension it has come to be applied unthinkingly to all who follow a spiritual path. In fact, it crystallizes the Reformation revolt against traditional Christian monasticism. Indeed, even before the high tide of the Reformation, the anonymous fourteenth-century author of *The Cloud of Unknowing* spoke regretfully of it in terms of Martha's complaint against Mary. Just as Martha complained about Mary, her sister, well-meaning people still misunderstand the contemplative approach. In terms of the Gospel story, this attitude of mind means that Martha chose the better way.

What would happen if everyone chose the contemplative approach? The first and most obvious answer is that it is an unreal question, since not everyone will do that, for there are more Marthas than Marys in the world. A deeper answer is that "Man does not live by bread alone." Everyone acts as a transmitting station of harmonious or destructive influences. The discordant, aggressive, or corrupt tendencies in people can be just as infectious as physical diseases, despite the fact that they may outwardly be doing social work. Conversely, the beneficent presence of spiritual people can have a harmonizing effect on all around, even if one never speaks with them or meets them face-to-face, even though they may be recluses with no apparent contact with the world. If people can believe that a musician bestows something on the community, though not supplying food or clothing, it is perhaps a step further to understand that spiritual people can, too. Indeed, their benefit is more powerful since, being independent of form, it can penetrate the mind directly without the mediation of the senses. For this reason, people have always sought out the fellowship of saints.

Their influence may be almost too subtle to perceive, like a vague perfume of roses, or it may be strong and tangible:

> Great souls, wherever they are, create a spiritual zone around them: and anybody coming within that zone realizes something like an electric current passing into him. It is a very strange phenomenon, impossible to explain, unless one has experienced it oneself.
>
> —*Spiritual Discourses of Swami Vijnanananda*,
> The Ramakrishna Math

In the subtler sense of giving spiritual aid, this error of turning outwards to the welfare of others instead of attending first to one's own quest goes right back to the foundation of *Mahayana* Buddhism some two thousand years ago. I do not question the spiritual potency of the *Mahayana*. The test of a tree is its fruit, and the great *Mahayana* sages have proved admirably that the way they trod was valid. That is all we need to know about a path—that it can take us to the goal. Nevertheless, their criticism of the *Hinayana* and their substitution of the *Bodhisattva* ideal for that of the *Arhat* expresses the viewpoint of ignorance.

Briefly, says the *Mahayana,* the *Arhat* seeks only private, individual Realization or *Nirvana*, whereas the *Bodhisattva* pledges to seek the Realization of all humankind and even holds back voluntarily from the final step of entering *Nirvana* until the self-imposed task of helping others has been accomplished.

Now, in the first place, there is no such thing as individual Realization. Realization means to realize that there is no individual. That is to say, it involves realization of the basic Buddhist doctrine of *anatta* (no-ego). *Nirvana* is that state which remains when the individual ceases to exist. How, then, can it be individual? To ask one who has awakened from the dream of individual being into the reality of *Nirvana* whether others also have attained Realization would be, as Maharshi expressed it, "as senseless as asking someone who wakes up from a dream whether the other people in the dream have also awakened."

Of course, *Mahayana* teachers fully understood this, but not all of their followers did. After speaking of the boundless compassion of the Buddha, one of their basic scriptures, as a safeguard, expressly affirms that there are no others to help:

> The famous *Diamond Sutra* makes it quite clear that the doctrine of compassion is only a facade for the ignorant, since in reality there are no others to whom to be compassionate; The Lord Buddha continued: "Do not think, *Subhuti*, that the *Tathagata* would consider within himself, 'I will deliver human beings.'" That would be a degrading thought. Why? Because there really are no sentient beings to be delivered by the *Tathagata*. Should there be any sentient being to be delivered by the *Tathagata*, it would mean that the *Tathagata* was cherishing within his mind arbitrary conceptions of phenomena such as one's own self, other selves, living beings, and a universal self. Even when the *Tathagata* refers to himself, he is not holding within his mind any such arbitrary thought. Only terres-

> trial human beings think of selfhood as being a personal possession (*Subhut*). Even the expression "terrestrial beings," as used by the *Tathagata,* does not mean that there are any such beings. It is only used as a figure of speech.
> —*Buddhism and Christianity in the Light of Hinduism*, by Arthur Osborne

As long as there is the concept of an "I," there is a concept of others. As long as there are others to help, there is an "I" to help them and therefore no Self-realization. The two go together; they cannot be separated.

Others
What will they think of this?
What will they say to that?
So others arise.
When there are others there's I.
In truth there just IS.
Isness alone is;
No others, no I, only a dance, a rhythm,
Only a being.

Of course, one has to play the game of "I and others," acting as though they existed. It is as if (as can sometimes happen) one had a dream and took part in its events while at the same time being awake enough to know that it was a dream.

What, then, is this vow to help others before seeking one's own Realization? Nothing but a resolve to remain in a state of ignorance (*avidya*). And how will that help others? It means clinging to the ego one has sworn to dissolve, regarding it as supremely wise and beneficent! In the language of theism, it reveals an overwhelming arrogance, the decision to show God how to run His world or to run it for Him.

Whatever may have been the traditional *Mahayana* discipline, this urge to help others by being a guru before one's time is one of the greatest pitfalls for the aspirant today. According to Milarepa, one of the great *Mahayana* saints,

> One should not be over hasty in setting out to help others before one has realized the Truth; if one does, it is a case of the blind leading the blind.
>
> —*The Life of Milarepa, Tibet's Great Yogi*,
> by Lobzang Jivaka and John Murray

We may find some compassion in vowing to help others, but more likely we will find more vanity and egoism. Few things so flatter the ego as the dream of being a guru surrounded by the adulation of disciples. Few things so impede an aspirant as turning one's energy outwards to guide others when it should still be turned inwards to oneself. In spiritual things it is true, as the nineteenth-century economists falsely asserted about material things, that you help others most by helping yourself. Maharshi never indulged such people. He told them, "Help yourself first before you think of helping others."

In any case, there is no need for any vow of compassion. The nearer a person comes to the truth of the Universal Self, the more one's phenomenal, individual self will take its true form. Without any vows, without arrogating to oneself the control of one's own destiny, we will act according to our innate nature, in a true way. It may not be one's function as a guru at all. If one becomes a guru, it will come about naturally and healthily when the time is ripe, without trying to force it.

A few examples will illustrate this. Buddha was the only son of his father and the heir apparent to his father's small kingdom. In what unctuous do-gooders would call "selfish" preoccupation with his own spiritual welfare, he abandoned wife and child, father and throne, and set forth alone as a *sadhu* to seek Enlightenment. Moreover, how many millions have since drawn sustenance from his renunciation? St. Francis of Assisi forsook the family business and alienated his father in order to embrace "Lady Poverty." What spiritual wealth has flowed forth from his material destitution! Sri Ramakrishna was consumed with ecstatic craving for the grace of the Divine Mother. Nothing else concerned him, neither helping himself or others. It seemed he would go mad with longing and despair. Then, when he did at last attain Enlightenment, such power flowed through him as to launch the spiritual regeneration of Hinduism and an attraction for Western seekers. Realization descended unsought on Ramana Maharshi when he was a schoolboy of seventeen. He left home, seeking only solitude, and remained immersed in the bliss of Being. Yet disciples gathered around, and he became one of the great sages of his time, through whom a uniquely direct path, adapted to the conditions of our age, was made accessible to seekers of truth.

All of which goes to show that the Universal Harmony does not require planning by anyone to give it shape. In theistic language, God can do His job without our advice.

Karma Marga

It is not meant that one should run from house and home, from wife and children and kindred, and flee out of the world, or forsake his goods so as not to regard them; but he must kill and make as nothing his own self-will.
—Jacob Boehme, *Mysterium Magnum* (12.55)

People today often think of *Karma Marga* as more or less equivalent to social service and, therefore, the most suited path to modern times, but, actually, this is a misconception. As originally understood, it meant the path of ritualistic action such as austerities, formal worship, breath-control, and recitation. In this sense, *Karma Marga* is the least, not the most, suited to modern conditions. Whether aspirants seek the goal through knowledge or devotion, few nowadays put their faith in ritualistic activity.

In its original form, *Karma Marga* can prepare us for the assault on the final peak, but it cannot make that assault. It must always fall short for the simple reason that action cannot transcend action, just as thought cannot transcend thought, and just as philosophy may help a person conceive of the goal but can never carry one to it.

What is referred to as *Karma Marga* today is actually an integration of *Karma Marga* with either *Jnana Marga* or *Bhakti Marga*. Modern people tend to practice this approach in the life of the world, which is a legitimate adaptation to the times.

Maharshi supported the integration of *Karma Marga* with *Jnana Marga*. In ancient times, Self-inquiry was a path for the renunciate, to be practiced in silence and solitude. When Maharshi readapted it to suit conditions of our time, he instructed people to practice it while continuing their work in the world, coolly and harmoniously, without grasping or self-interest, without even the idea "I am doing this."

> There is no principle that actions can be performed only on the basis of the "I-am-the-doer" idea, and therefore there is no reason to ask whether they can be performed and the duties discharged without that idea. To take a common example, an accountant working all day in his office and scrupulously attending to his duties might seem to the spectator to be shouldering all the financial responsibilities of

> the institution. But, knowing that he is not personally affected by the in-take or out-going, he remains unattached and free from the "I-am-the-doer" feeling in doing his work, while at the same time he does it perfectly well. In the same way, it is quite possible for the wise householder who earnestly seeks Liberation to discharge his duties in life (which, after all, are his destiny) without any attachment, regarding himself merely as an instrument for the purpose. Such activity is not an obstacle on the path to Knowledge, nor does Knowledge prevent a one from discharging duties in life. Knowledge and activity are never mutually antagonistic and the realization of one does not impede the performance of the other, nor does performance of the one affect the realization of the other.
>
> —*The Teachings of Ramana Maharshi in His Own Words*

This is in conformity with the teaching of the *Bhagavad Gita*:

> Your concern is only with action, not with its results. Do not be motivated by the fruit of action, but also do not cling to inaction. (2.47)

So, also, is Maharshi's warning that you cannot find peace by mere physical renunciation, because whatever outer changes you may make in your life, your mind still remains with you, and this has to be subdued. The following *Gita* verses confirm this:

> No one can remain really actionless, even for an instant, for everyone is driven inevitably to action by the qualities (*gunas*) born of nature. (3.5)

Outer renunciation, as Maharshi warned, is seldom advisable. When it involves shirking of duties, it is actually pernicious:

> Renunciation of duties is not right. It is prompted by ignorance and is said to be *tamasic*. (18.7)
>
> That renunciation is regarded as pure, which consists in performing duties, because they ought to be performed, while renouncing attachment and the fruit of one's actions. (18.9)

What does this involve in practice? Not social service. People who follow this path do not go out of their way to find and relieve social injustices or cases of ignorance, poverty, and disease. On the other hand, they do not cause injustice or disharmony. They help to the best of their ability when someone needing help comes their way. They accomplish their work in life, both professionally and at home, as a function, a duty, a harmony, interjecting their self-will as little as possible. By being harmonious, they diffuse harmony.

We can call this path as prescribed by Ramana Maharshi the contemporary form of *Jnana Marga*, but since it is performed in the midst of life's activities, we can also call it a revised form of *Karma Marga*.

The late Swami Ramdas is an outstanding example of the fusion of *Karma Marga* and *Bhakti Marga*. In his early autobiography, *In Quest of God*, he recalls how he traveled about India as a penniless *sadhu*, visiting ashrams and Swamis; wandering through the Himalayas; living in caves; traveling ticketless on trains, bullied by railway officials and police. He spent all of his time repeating the name of *Ram* and seeing *Ram* manifested in all who met him, frie[illegible] or hostile. If one *sadhu* gave him a drinkin[illegible] [illegible]er stole it, he would simply say R[illegible] [illegible]in another took it away. [illegible] up an ashram, he would [illegible]*am*" and to women as [illegible]

[illegible]s to see God manifested [illegible] love God in loving [illegible] service, since whom[illegible] [illegible]ined by *Ram*, or the Divine. [illegible] sanction this attitude, too. Christ sanctioned [illegible]ying, "Inasmuch as you do it to one of the least of these you do it also to me." This attitude would seem to be totally alien to Islam, which does not acknowledge the possibility of Divine Incarnation, and yet the *Koran* teaches, "Whichever way you turn there is the Face of God." (2.115) In the face of each person, the *bhakta* sees a mask over the Face of God.

Whichever kind of *Karma Marga* may be followed, it raises the question of work or renunciation, an active or contemplative life. It is a mistake to suppose that most monks are contemplative. Most Christian monasteries divide the day into periods of manual labor, study, prayer, and ritual worship, leaving little time for leisure and not a great deal for sleep. In a Buddhist monastery, a monk's time is usually fully occupied. Zen monasteries, too, in particular, tend to prescribe hard, manual labor for the monk's.

A Hindu ashram is a less formal institution. Properly speaking, it is simply the colony that grows up around a guru, and therefore its character will vary with that of the guru in charge.

Therefore, in some ashrams the discipline is rather lax, while in others it is quite strict. Occupational work may or may not be demanded of the residents. They may be required to carry on the entire maintenance of the ashram, growing crops, preparing food, etc. Some ashrams even require the recruits to surrender their entire property to it, remaining as dependents like monks in a monastery. One difference is that visitors and temporary residents are usually allowed to visit an ashram, seldom at a monastery. They may or may not be subject to the same discipline as the regular residents.

In its lack of formal routine, Sri Ramanasramam is rather exceptional. Ramana Maharshi himself never organized an ashram. The necessary framework was constructed around him—a meditation hall, an office and bookstall, a dining hall, post office, dispensary, etc. A number of *sadhus* settled there and worked at one job or another—librarian, postmaster, cook, typist, gardener—all the varied occupations necessary for running an institution. Other *sadhus* settled down outside the Ashram, neither working for it nor maintained by it. Married couples built houses, establishing a colony around the Ashram. What they did with their time was their own affair. Such *sadhus* and householders count as members of the Ashram insofar as they are devotees of Bhagavan and obey the Ashram rules while on its premises, but the arrangement of their lives outside is up to them, as is also their maintenance.

This rather anomalous category of devotees raises the question of renunciation. When a Christian renounces the world, such a person normally enters a monastery. One no longer has property or family, nor any material insecurity. The monastery provides food, clothing, and shelter—all that one needs. Much the same applies to a Buddhist monk, although the monk may be obliged to go out to beg for food, thereby contributing to the upkeep of the monastery, while participating in traditional monastic discipline. The monastic routine also shelters the monk from mental insecurity that comes from lack of regular occupation.

The position of a Hindu *sadhu* or *sannyasin* is quite different. On renouncing property, family, and caste, he becomes a homeless wanderer. Nobody is responsible for his maintenance. He is expected to wander, begging for food and accepting whatever is given. If his presence makes a strong impression, followers may gather around him and attend to his needs. If he has some skill that is valued, he may accept food and shelter from an ashram in exchange for his services. He may even accept an allowance from his former family or from some benevolent householder but, generally, he has no material security, no routine of life, and no regular occupation.

During Maharshi's lifetime, one often heard people ask his permission to renounce the world and go forth as *sadhus*, but I never once heard him consent:

> Why do you think you are a householder? The similar thought that you are a *sannyasi* will haunt you even if you go forth as one. Whether you continue in the household or renounce it and go to live in the forest, your mind haunts you. The ego is the source of thought. It creates the body and world and makes you think of being a householder. If you renounce it [your home life], it will only substitute the thought of renunciation for that of the family, and the environment of the forest for that of the household. But the mental obstacles are always there for you. They even

> increase greatly in the new surroundings. Change of environment is no help. The one obstacle is the mind, and this must be overcome whether in the home or in the forest. If you can achieve this in the forest, why not in the home? So why change the environment? Your efforts can be made even now, whatever be the environment.
>
> —*The Teachings of Ramana Maharshi in His Own Words*

Notice that Bhagavan did not say, "The mental obstacles remain the same for you in the new surroundings," but "They even increase greatly in the new surroundings." In fact, I have seen a number of sad cases of this. A person's professional work keeps the mind occupied on the surface while at the same time permitting an undercurrent of remembering or meditation. Bhagavan urged people to foster this undercurrent, to do one's work impersonally, asking oneself, "Who does this work? Who am I?" As an illustration, he spoke about the actor who plays his part on the stage quite well, although knowing at heart that he is not the person he acts. Therefore, the actor does not get elated if the playwright has allotted that person final success, or dejected if he has allotted failure or a tragic death.

A person's professional work may be irksome; it often is. One may feel disappointed at how much more progress could be made if the whole day was free for spiritual practice. But before taking the drastic step of renouncing life in the world, one should try to occupy the mind exclusively with meditation or whatever spiritual practice one performs from the time of waking in the morning until sleep can no longer be held off at night. One will find that one cannot hold the mind persistently to the quest even for one whole day. Only at a high level of development does the mind cease to demand outer activity. Deprived of the irksome but relatively harmless activity of professional work, it will turn instead to more injurious activities such as daydreaming, planning, scheming, or social trivialities and, as Maharshi said, the mental obstacles will "increase greatly."

Nor can we fill the gap by reading. We may find a certain amount of reading helpful and, in many cases, necessary, especially at the beginning, but excessive reading can become a drug, dulling the mind and distracting from real spiritual effort. Once the mind is convinced of the basic truth of Identity, why reconvince it over and over again? Why study techniques that one is not going to use; theories that one does not need? Sometimes something one reads may come as a useful reminder and spur one on to greater or wiser effort, but much of it acts just like a drug to keep the mind occupied. Reading may even lead to gluttony for useless facts, pride in possession of them, or arrogance at the thought of understanding more than the writer.

Family ties may also seem irksome. It may appear that one would have a freer mind for *sadhana* without them. Yet, in most cases, we can make family life a discipline for subduing egoism, which is the purpose of *sadhana*. Removing family ties all too often invites an upsurge of egoism, leaving a person free to think exclusively of oneself—the impression one is making on others, one's progress on the path, even one's physical health and material needs.

Of course, if a *sannyasin* really renounces everything and has to beg and cook his food, that may prove occupation enough, though not necessarily a nobler or more spiritually profitable activity than that which he has renounced. If, however, one retains sufficient means of subsistence to escape this and the mind remains without any occupation other than *sadhana*, there is grave danger of deterioration. Desire, which one may rashly thought to have conquered, may rise again. One may also fill the gap by setting oneself up as a guide to others when one should still be concentrating on one's own progress. One may fall victim to undesirable activity or come under the domination of a false guide. Finally, one may simply sink into boredom and trivialities from which one will eventually seek escape by renouncing the quest entirely. One who has seen so many cases of renunciation leading to deterioration can only advise people earnestly to refrain and put up with the irksome but protective outer shell of professional and family life.

Moreover, spiritual growth, like the growth of a seed, takes place in the dark. Grace sinks down into it like gentle rain. Progress may be the greatest when least visible, even when one is dejected and thinks one is falling back. To strip away the outer cover of routine life and try to subject ourselves to the full, day-long glare of the conscious mind may do us incalculable harm. From this point of view, also, it is better not to renounce.

This caution, however, does not apply to Christians or Buddhists thinking of becoming monks since, as I said above, the monastic routine of life is, in most cases, quite an active *Karma Marga*, whether in the original or the modern meaning of the word.

Ahad

Before the beginning He was,
Beyond the ending He is,
Hidden in the heart of man,
Flared forth in a myriad stars and a bird's song.

Unchanged and unbegun,
Unfellowed, He, the One,
The All He is, the Alone,
Otherness but a dream gone on too long.

Realization and Guidance

Once we perceive that effort and a guide are needed in the quest of life's goal, the question arises, whichever path one may follow, whether the guide need be a realized person or not.

Strange as it may sound, there is no necessary connection between a person's state of inner illumination and the grace that flows through that being to strengthen and inspire others. In fact, such grace may not flow through realized beings, in which case their high state will not be recognized. It is simply not their function, nature, or destiny (whichever term one may use) to guide others. Indeed, Bhagavan would sometimes say of wandering beggars or *sadhus*, "How do we know who comes to us in their form?" This implies that it is not a person's inner state that is recognizable, but the dynamic effect of that state. The state remains the same whether a dynamic effect flows from it or not.

Naturally, it is not easy to give examples of this, for the simple reason that such a person would remain unknown. Two cases do come to mind. One is Christ before he set forth on his mission. According to Christian doctrine, he was born without original sin, that is to say, Self-realized from birth. And yet no one in his hometown felt that he was a holy man, no crowds flocked to him, no disciples sought him out, no power flowed through him to effect cures. In fact, when he went back there later, his fellow townsmen were incredulous that the local carpenter's boy should have turned into a prophet (which confirms, incidentally, that he had spent his youth there and that they did know him as the local carpenter's boy). The other is Maharshi. Realization descended on him spontaneously when he was still a schoolboy, but nobody perceived his changed state, either at home or at school. Only later, when power flowed through him and disciples began to gather around, did people recognize him for what he was.

Grace and power can also flow through one who is not realized. How many powerful religious leaders—the Wesleys and Luthers of history—have inspired others and led great movements without any claim to higher understanding or inner development? Clearly, in many such cases, the grace of God has worked through them. However, spiritual guidance of the aspirant, which is in a different category, requires mystical knowledge and insight. Here, too, can the unrealized person act aright through grace? To some extent, yes. It is difficult to find examples, since followers of such a one are likely to claim that the person is realized. I shall take as an example Swami Vivekananda. On the one hand, his followers claim realization for him, while on the other hand, some critics are so derogatory as to deny that he was even rightly guided. In fact, one of them declares that Ramakrishna was deluded by his infatuation for Vivekananda. Let us examine the case.

Sri Ramakrishna was enthusiastic about Narendra Dutt, the future Vivekananda, and spoke of him as the person destined to carry on his work of restoring vigor to a languishing, almost decadent Hinduism. By the touch of his hands, he induced in Naren a pre-vision of realization. When this experience ended, he said, "Now I am going to lock it up in a box and you will have to go out and do your work without it. But when your work is finished the Mother will give it back to you." Records of Vivekananda's last days, when he had withdrawn from all active work, show that realization did indeed come to him, and he saw dispassionately and objectively some of the shortcomings in his life's work.

Here we have a picture equally far from a Self-realized Vivekananda and a deluded and infatuated Ramakrishna. This picture implies that Ramakrishna's work was to be carried on by one from whom Realization was to be withheld until the work was accomplished, very much like the *Mahayana* ideal of the *Bodhisattva*.

There is no doubt about the grace that flowed through Vivekananda. After his death, the Mother, Sarada Devi, said of him:

What powers did Naren Swami have by himself? It was

because God acted through him that he achieved what he did.
—*At Holy Mother's Feet*, Advaita Ashram

At the famous Chicago Parliament of Religions—famous now only because he took part in it—it was his presence, not his arguments, that impressed people. He had got no further than, "Sisters and brothers of America!" when a torrent of applause swept the hall. From that point on, in speech after speech, contact after contact, people felt the power and grace in him. A published book of tributes (*Reminiscences of Swami Vivekananda*, Advaita Ashram) by thirty of his Hindu and Western admirers shows the overpowering impression he made on people, the support they derived from him, and the simplicity and humor that he maintained despite their adulation.

Nevertheless, to say in general that the guru need not be realized would be to simplify the question far too much. In the first place, it is usually harmful for a person to set up as a guru before having attained realization. It impedes one's further progress on the path by turning energy outward to guide others when it should still be turned inward to one's own *sadhana*. If not impossible for such a person to make further progress, it is at least much more difficult. Not only that, there is danger of latent egoism being revived, bringing one to a worse state than before. If the ego still exists, it may lie low for a while, facilitating the flow of grace, and then rise up and turn this to its own service, poisoning it in the process. Moreover, there is the danger of hypocrisy and arrogance. So sweet is adulation to the ego that one is likely to allow disciples to treat the "Master" as a realized person when merited or not, which is hypocrisy. Alternatively, one may become arrogant and overbearing, crave flattery, refuse to listen to criticism, and shout down arguments. It is foolish to invite such dangers, which few can withstand. As a footnote, Vivekananda withstood these temptations, perhaps because he passed on all the homage he received to his master, and perhaps because he received Sri Ramakrishna's unseen protection. If he had not withstood the dangers, he could not have attained ultimate Realization.

And what about the disciples of an unrealized guru? In former times in India, both Hindus and Muslims normally received initiation from a kind of family guru, and something of this tradition still remains. However, this practice produces only a low order of potency, whether for good or evil—perhaps not much more than confirmation in a Christian church. The disciple does not seek realization nor does the guru claim it.

However, those who seek a guru in their quest for Realization must understand that no one teacher can guide others further than that person has gone. Therefore, an unrealized guru would not be of much use at best. There is even a danger that the guru's faults of character may be transmitted to the disciples. In general, any sickness of character is as infectious as a physical disease. Thus, masters lay great emphasis on the company disciples keep, urging people to seek out the wise and pure and to shun the evil-minded. Moreover, disciples open themselves to the influence of their guru much more than to anyone else. To submit to a guru who has developed the vices of hypocrisy or arrogance, or any other manifestations of a resurgent ego, is as foolhardy as one that takes a wife or husband who has tuberculosis; there is little likelihood of escaping infection.

René Guenon likened the influence flowing through a spiritual functionary of any sort to the electric current flowing through a wire, unaffected by the cleanliness or otherwise of the wire. It would be more apt to compare it to water flowing through a pipe to a thirsty person. If the pipe is filthy inside, the water will quench one's thirst just the same, but it will probably transmit typhoid or cholera in the process. Seekers should weigh the dangers against the advantages very carefully before accepting a guru.

The matter is further complicated by the question of what is meant by "realization." Bhagavan stated categorically that there are no stages of Self-realization. Either you have realized the Self or you have not. By Self-realization, he meant the dissolution of the illusory ego-sense and its replacement by constant, conscious identity with the Universal Self or pure Being. He lived constantly in that state, which is the ultimate. There is nothing beyond it—here, one does not go into *samadhi*, for he is always in *samadhi*, whether with outer awareness or not. The realized sage makes no prayer, for who is to pray to whom? Similarly, there is no revelation, for who is to reveal to whom?

But this is a very rare state. There are two kinds of approximation to it. One person has a theoretical understanding of Identity, fortified by a more or less constant inner, nontheoretical remembrance and by occasional glimpses of realized Identity. The writings of such great mystic philosophers as Plotinus and Eckhart reveal seekers in this category. Bhagavan's disciples take this path of approach, although such a state cannot be called realization.

Some of Bhagavan's disciples did act as gurus even in his

lifetime. He did not forbid it. If asked whether a person could act as a guru before attaining realization, he would more likely reply noncommittally, "If it is a person's destiny to be a Guru he will." But he did at times warn against it. Generally, he made it clear that it is better and safer to concentrate on one's own *sadhana* than to try to guide others.

Nor is there anything egoistic about doing so. (How can there be anything egoistic about trying to uproot the ego?) Silent, invisible influences are far more potent than the average person may imagine. Whether the spiritual wayfarer gives formal guidance to others or not, the influence that radiates from a person will affect others. The greater one's purity, the more free one is from the ambition to teach others. Therefore, the more beneficent will be one's influence. Maharshi is the Guru of all who turn to him in their heart, now as in his body's lifetime. Consequently, no intermediate guru is needed.

The other type of approximation comes through the actualization of latent powers and realization of higher states of being. Less direct spiritual paths may lead to this, such as *yogic* and *tantric* paths in Hinduism, and *Hermetic* paths in medieval Christianity and Islam, to name a few. This is far more complicated. Such a path may lead through successive stages, each one requiring a new initiation and leading to a new "realization"—not Self-realization but the realization of some higher state. This type of path also may or may not be illuminated by pre-glimpses of its goal; it may or may not involve states of ecstasy. Those unaware of spiritual truth may simplify things far too much in conceiving only of a physical world and a spiritual worldlessness. There is a vast luxuriance of intermediary states, just as there are physical forms of life between a human being and stone. *Advaitins* also simplify things, but deliberately, in closing their eyes to all intermediate states with their powers and experiences to avoid the danger of being distracted from the goal of Self-realization. But there are paths and teachings that lead stage by stage through the complexity. The Hermeticists had their graded heavens; the Sufis have a series of *maqamat,* or stages of realization; Buddhists also speak of stages. Clearly, many Christian saints may not have had actual realization or even theoretical understanding of the ultimate truth of Identity. Nevertheless, they had the ability of guiding aspirants.

Similarly, there is no reason for presuming that prophets in the Semitic tradition may have been in a permanent state of realized Identity. Rather, the Hebrew and Islamic scriptures suggest that they were not, nor was it was not necessary for the work they had to do within their traditions. For instance, the so-called "chariot mysticism" of the Old Testament Prophets obviously focuses on the realm of duality, of seeing, not being. The *Koran,* in particular, insists that prophets are just people who have been called to a particularly responsible but onerous undertaking. Mohammed himself declared that he experienced a time with God in which no angel or inspired prophet was equal to him. Though we may strain language unjustifiably to suggest that this implies realized identity, he did, however, add that this was not his normal state, but one that was experienced on occasion.

Let us again consider these two approaches to Self-realization, which reflect a constant, conscious abidance in a state of Identity. Those who have attained stabilization at some point on the spiritual path, even though the summit may remain obscured from sight, (and they may not know that there is one), have acquired certain abilities, which can be competently used. Perhaps the ability to act as a guru is among them. It is possible that in the organization to which they belong, using the technique which they have mastered, they will be able to guide others to the position in which they abide.

Reincarnation

Any discussion of rebirth takes place only from the point of view of ignorance, because from the point of view of Knowledge, there is no one to be reborn. Therefore, Bhagavan would generally brush the question aside when asked about it. He would often reply, saying, "First find out whether you are born now before asking whether you will be reborn." Or, "Why worry what you will be after death before you know what you are now?"

The one thing that all of us are absolutely certain about is our own existence. We may come to believe that the world outside us is real or unreal; that we are sitting at a solid table, or at a cluster of whirling electrons as the nuclear scientists tell us; that there is or is not a God; that other people really exist or that they are imagined by us like the people we saw in last night's dream. However, what we know from personal, first-hand experience is that we exist.

From this apparent certainty, we make a wholly unwarranted deduction: that we are a limited individual being, identical with or located in a particular body/mind instrument. Therefore, we start to worry about what will happen to this hypothetical individual when, at death, the body/mind instrument dissolves. Will it continue to exist without a body? Will it get an ethereal body in place of a physical one? Or, will it take form as a new identity in a new physical body? It is no use asking the *Jnani*, since an enlightened being knows that these are unreal questions, for the hypothetical individual about whom they are asked never really existed.

The unreality of the theoretical individual, the basic doctrine of *anatta*, or no-ego, forms the very starting point of Buddhism. Its final realization is the culmination of all religion. A religion like Christianity, which does not say outright that the ego does not exist and never has, comes around to the same point by insisting that it must be sacrificed. When you give up your life (the ego) for Christ's sake, you will find it (the true, universal life of the Spirit); whereas, when you cling to it, you will lose it.

But to give it up is the hardest thing to do, even though one may be convinced theoretically of its unreality. People cling so tenaciously to the false hypothesis of individual being that religions have to lead them by any manner of ways to weaken this belief by attacking it, cutting away its roots of desire, and by curbing its exuberant growth of indulgence. Religions call the ways of indulging the ego "vices" and ban them; they also call the ways of curbing the ego "virtues" and extol them. Indeed, all religions agree on this one point: the need to discipline or deny the ego. Those who renounce religion often share one common feature in the name of self-expression—indulgence of the ego.

This preoccupation with the hypothetical individual has even invaded religion, taking the form of wondering what will happen to the self after death. Indeed, for many people, religion means sharing beliefs and opinions about what will happen after death. Really, this issue plays an insignificant part in religion; in fact, two of the world's great religions, Judaism and the original Taoism, do not stress this point. By overly exaggerating the importance of the apparent individual, a risky spiritual passivity has taken hold. By focusing on an afterlife existence, religion comes to signify, "What will happen to me?" instead of "What have I to achieve?"

The act of dying will not of itself destroy the ego-illusion. The body is not the obstacle to *Nirvana* or Realization, whichever one may call it, but rather the "I-am-the-body" idea. Therefore, Bhagavan affirmed that there is no difference between realization in the body and realization after the death of the body. If the ego-illusion remains until the end of one's life, death will not destroy it. On the other hand, if it is already liquidated, death will not revive it.

Since it is only the hypothetical individual or illusory ego that can undergo reincarnation, the question exists, as said previously, only from the "point of view of ignorance." That does not imply that it is completely invalid, since posthumous states of being, though no more real than this life, are no less real, also. It is best to wake up from the whole series of dreams, but for those who are unable to do so, it is possible to describe their sequence. Nor is doing this a mere concession to curiosity. It has a positive value within its limited range of reality, since the dream-sequence, as long as it lasts, is shaped by karma, the law of cause and effect. People certainly benefit from understanding that what they do in this life shapes what they will be, and what they will undergo subsequently.

The many religions generally agree that those who have failed to awaken to Reality pass on from this life to a subtle state in which they reap the harvest of good or ill that they have sown. The impressions preserved in the subconscious arise to form the environment and substance of a new world, just as they do during a dream. Therefore, the experiences of heaven and hell arise.

Eastern teachers add, however, that this is not the end. How can it be? How could an individual state of reaping the harvest of a phenomenal life be frozen into perpetuity? After having enjoyed or suffered what has been accumulated, the person is born again into a new life, starting at the level to which he or she had risen or fallen in the previous one; and in this new life, the person again will sow a harvest that later will have to be reaped.

In general, there is no more rebirth for those who have awakened from the dream of individual being into the reality of Universal Being. However, we should never believe something just because it is widely accepted. That leads to arguments about doctrine. It is better to understand why it is said.

There is a twofold pattern of manifestation. Pure Being,

which in essence we are, is manifested horizontally and vertically through space and time. Horizontally, it takes form as all the other beings of our present world, while vertically, it appears as all the past and future incarnations of our present person. We stand at the intersection of the two patterns.

But when we realize our identity with pure Being (which is manifest in this entire panorama), and when even in this lifetime we cease to consider the body we identify with as "ours," or to suffer its destiny, we find it impossible to consider any other body or lifetime "ours," too, now or in any other time or place. I say "other" rather than "future," for the word "future" would reintroduce the idea of temporal succession and causation, which has to be transcended. To be embodied, then, is an action of the entire universe, since we are identical with the One Self, of which all this is a manifestation.

We may look at other appearances—threads in the world tapestry—which our body is, and say "I." We may say that it has been, will be, or has performed some function, but all this is from the point of view of the onlooker. If we also say that there is no incarnation, present or future, or that the whole world is our incarnation, there is no contradiction. We must remember that an "individual" does not become free from reincarnation at the moment of Realization, but realizes that he was never bound by it.

The Problem of Suffering

Some theorists are perplexed by what they call "the problem of suffering." The philosopher Hume even thought he had discovered in it a weapon to destroy religion. God, he argued, in order to be God, must be both good and omnipotent, but the existence of suffering proves that God either does not want to prevent it or is unable to, which is to say that God is either not good or not omnipotent, and in either case is not God. Therefore, there is no God.

Certainly one can agree that there is no anthropomorphic God of the sort that Hume envisaged, no kind, old man sitting in a back room, working out people's destinies and allotting rewards and punishments. There is no God with a human scale of values; no God made in the likeness of humankind. To postulate such a God would mean that the object of human life is mundane happiness, and God's job is to ensure it. There are people who get through life with no great suffering—no actual hunger, no lack of clothing or shelter, reasonable security, fairly friendly relations with those around them, few long or painful illnesses, and finally, death while sleeping. Is that the perfect life? If God could arrange for everyone to get by as easily as that, would He have done his job? Would He be accepted by such critics? Then why did Christ tell some of his followers to give up their possessions and become mendicants? Why did he draw people to a life in which, he warned them, they would be persecuted and even killed? Obviously, he had a totally different conception of values.

The question of suffering is bound up with the question of values, and this is dependent on the meaning or purpose of life. Do those who complain of suffering recognize any meaning or purpose at all? If their aim is not merely to get by without too much hardship, what is it? To serve others? That would mean to help others get by without too much hardship, so that ultimately it comes to the same thing. Is there anything for which it is ultimately worthwhile to face suffering? If not, life would indeed be dismal. The answer is contained in a brief description of a foreglimpse of Reality by a person with no doctrinal understanding. During the birth anniversary of Ramana Maharshi, on a roof terrace in Calcutta, among those present was a teenage girl who, as she sat in meditation, people saw an expression of radiant serenity. Later she put her experience in words, as far as it is possible:

> I am not the mind, nor the body—found myself in the Heart; that me that lives after death. There was breathtaking joy in the feeling "I-am," the greatest possible earthly joy, the full enjoyment of existence. No way to describe it—the difference between this joy and complete happiness of the mind is greater than between the blackest misery and the fullest elation of the mind. Gradually—rapidly—my body seemed to be expanding from the Heart. It engulfed the whole universe. It didn't feel anymore. The only real thing was God. I could not identify myself as any speck in that vastness—nor other people—there was only God, nothing but God. The word "I" had no meaning anymore; it meant the whole universe—everything is God, the only Reality.

What prevents this glorious happiness from being one's normal state? Obviously, it is the ego, with its attachment to things of the world. Therefore, the ego veils true happiness and is the cause of suffering. That is the sane and realistic approach. Actually, this belief forms the basis of Buddhism: Suffering exists, it is due to desire, and it can therefore be eliminated by the eradicating of desire. The Buddha's understanding is a clear reading of the law of cause and effect. The other attitude means clinging to the cause while expecting some outside agency to shield one from the effect. And that is a pipe dream. As long as a person is attached to things, and primarily to the ego, it is futile to expect some outside agency to remove the frustration that attachment brings. The effect will follow the cause quite impersonally, as Buddha put it, "as the cartwheel follows the hooves of the bullock."

Once one conceives of joy, the difference between complete

happiness of the mind is greater than between the blackest misery and the fullest elation of the mind. It then becomes necessary to define "suffering," for happiness and suffering are not just quantitative but qualitative.

Presumably, imprisonment is a form of suffering, yet a monk's cell can be as austere as that of a prisoner. Certainly, the regime of fourth-century Christian anchorites in the Egyptian desert was far harsher than anything inflicted on modern prisoners, yet monks voluntarily chose it. Was it suffering? When Christ told his followers that they would be persecuted for his sake, was he inviting them to a life of suffering? It was not compulsory. Anyone who decided that the suffering outweighed the advantages was free to leave. As Shakespeare said, "There is nothing either good or bad but thinking makes it so." This profound truth must govern the definition of "suffering." If we defined it as "unwelcome distress," we could not speak of suffering concerning those who have truly surrendered to the Divine Will. Additionally, they never speak of it themselves. A person who is truly surrendered may undergo imprisonment, sickness, or persecution, but one never hears he or she complain or refer to it as "suffering."

Consider another kind of suffering: the self-inflicted suffering of asceticism that is undergone in the quest for divine grace. This does not have to be. What justifies asceticism—though not every ascetic realizes this—is that the blindness that makes a person mistake the unreal for the Real is emotionally motivated and can therefore be cured only by eradicating this motivation. Attachment to the ego makes one blind to the Spirit, which is another way of phrasing the basic truth of Buddhism, that desire is the cause of suffering. Someone who appreciates this will say quite naturally, "Very well, then, I will break my attachment to the ego by allowing it no indulgence of any sort, physical or mental. I will remain celibate, eschew company, and eat only the barest minimum—even unappetizing food." To say that this reaction is understandable does not mean that it can be counted on to attain the goal. The ego is extremely subtle and can resist the onslaught of outer discipline, even continuing to flourish, despite the blows that are directed at it. Its pride may even be transferred to asceticism, a pride in being more ascetic than one's colleagues. However, the contrary approach of remaining unattached to life's conveniences without renouncing external things can also not be counted, because here, too, the ego is very cunning. It may easily believe, "I am not attached to any specific indulgent behavior and can easily give it up if I wanted; consequently, there is no need to actually do so." But how is one to be sure of that unless one is put to the test?

Many of the saints and ascetics who followed Christ faced persecution, yet they had an active and enterprising attitude towards life. They had a higher goal and were prepared to pay the price for it. Those, on the other hand, who only complain of suffering, are passive towards life. All they ask is to get by with as little hardship as possible. And they consider that God ought to share their point of view and enable them to do this. This is very unrealistic.

Those who aspire to Enlightenment are realistic. As a by-product of their spiritual understanding, they help to relieve suffering in others. For just as suffering is mainly caused, directly or indirectly, by human egoism, so it is relieved by abnegation of the ego. Instead of sitting passively and expecting relief from a divine agency, spiritual seekers make themselves instruments through which divine power may flow. Becoming an instrument may be an intangible way through which peace and harmony emanate from within, acting as a healing balm upon those with whom they come into contact, while quite tangibly effecting spiritual healing and resolving distressing circumstances.

Even so, those who complain of suffering may still argue that much of it is not due to the egoism of the sufferer. It may be caused by what appears to them to be an act of God. For instance, a war of aggression by one country causes havoc and desolation in another; a crime by one person causes poverty and bereavement to another.

Although in such cases the suffering is not due to the sufferer's egoism, it still has its origins in attachment to the ego. Otherwise, a saint or sage who has transcended the ego would experience suffering associated with war or poverty, but they do not.

From a subordinate viewpoint, however, those who do not strive to overcome the ego and cannot bear to have it too severely buffeted confirms, as John Donne says, "No man is an island." Therefore, one suffers from another's egoism. We are all interconnected and cause one another's weal and woe. From this point of view, the world is under the regency of humankind, which has consistently made a mess of it, creating a purgatory out of what could be a paradise. As far back as it goes, history reveals a long record of wars and exploitation, slaughter, bereavement, human-made poverty, all due to egoism by which people bring suffering to others and, eventually, frustration to themselves; for no one, as the Buddha pointed out, can stave off old age, sickness, and death. The more people indulge their desires, the more they suffer from eventual denial, having inflicted suffering on others for their own gratification. Yet, even from this viewpoint, given people's capacity to create mischief, it is illogical for them to appeal to some external divine agency to cancel out the effect of the mischief. This condition applies to all of humanity: all of us undergo suffering because of desire and can eliminate suffering only by renouncing it.

There is another category of suffering not obviously provoked by the sufferer, which seems to stem from an "act of God," involving such apparently unmerited pain, such as sickness and poverty. This suffering is not bound up with one's neighbors, but rather with the whole series of one's past and future lives. In this case, the law of cause and effect works with flawless precision.

One steps onto the stage of life burdened with past karma. Any suffering one may undergo, although seemingly undeserved in this lifetime, lightens the load one will have to bear in future lives. Debts do not lapse; only Self-knowledge dissolves their cause. Otherwise, as Christ said, "They shall be paid to the uttermost farthing."

Then, is the whole round of successive births and deaths the suffering from which we seek to escape? That is precisely the Hindu and Buddhist doctrine, which is not in the least pessimistic. This doctrine does not mean that life is all suffering or even that suffering necessarily outweighs happiness, but simply that the ego is vulnerable to suffering. Additionally, pessimism is a sentimental attitude, whereas doctrine is a formulation of truth, so the two can have nothing in common.

Neither is the doctrine of optimism, for the same reason; but it is good news, which is better. There are paths that lead from the vulnerability of life to perpetual, timeless bliss, the difference between which was articulated by the young lady in Calcutta as, ". . . complete happiness of the mind is greater than between the blackest misery and the fullest elation of the mind."

Certainly the way for the wise and the valiant is to remove the causes of suffering in oneself, not to rail against God for allowing effect to follow cause.

Quest and Egoism

It is tremendously exhilarating to learn for the first time the truth of the One Self and the possibility of Self-realization. At last, life has meaning and purpose! All previous desires and ambitions fade into insignificance, since their fulfillment leads only to rearranged circumstances in the dream of earthly life. The quest, however, helps us penetrate through the dream mirage to reality. So one commits to the great quest and, most often, joins a group following some path or discipline. One looks with reverence upon the senior members, who are already advanced on the way. Soon, however, one discovers that not all of them merit this respect. A few seem earnest in their efforts and helpful towards others, but with a shock of disillusionment, the new recruit discovers many to be imperfect people. Not only have they failed to eradicate their faults, but they may act less kindly than associates or former associates in the everyday world. Spiritual aspirants sometimes speak as maliciously and act as jealously as everyone else. In addition, some are grasping and possessive, some assertive and boastful; some lack self-control, while others embellish their path with a string of cheap love affairs. If understanding and truth have awakened in the newcomer's heart, none of this behavior can deflect such a person from the quest through skepticism and doubt. Nevertheless, neophytes often experience great disappointment, and many have felt that it needs an explanation.

One explanation holds that the process of *sadhana* squeezes out the lower tendencies in a person and brings them to the surface in order to cast them out, just as psychoanalysis is meant to do. Although this process is essentially a healing one, it can cause a lot of difficulty and inconvenience for the aspirant and for those who have to live or work with this person. Someone once complained to Bhagavan that undesirable thoughts crowded into his mind when he was trying to meditate. Bhagavan responded, "That's all right. Everything that is in the mind has to be brought out. How can they be cast out if they are not brought to the surface?" On another occasion, someone complained to Bhagavan of the arrogant behavior of one of the senior devotees, and Maharshi said, "That is only his *vasanas* (inherent tendencies) coming out."

Sometimes our first perception of Truth has a transforming effect, bringing out all that is beautiful within us, so that our friends find us to be a new and delightful person. But that is only temporary. In the aftermath of awakening, our vast tendencies may surface. Those who marveled at our improvement may begin to find us worse than before and question whether it would not have been better had we never put our hand to the plough. At this point, the armies of our noble and regressive tendencies must enter into battle, which in fact may last a lifetime.

Even with this understanding, how do we explain the many cases of aspirants who were outright egoists before they took to the path and seem to remain so afterwards? Moreover, what of the good, kind-hearted people who do not take any path? When Christ was asked why he associated with riff-raff, he answered the sick need a doctor, not the healthy. There may have been some sarcasm in this statement, since one can hardly imagine that those who challenged Christ were spiritually healthy. Nevertheless, those who recognize that they are spiritually sick often seek treatment. That is why it is so often eccentrics and outsiders that become aspirants.

An American woman once asked Bhagavan why we should seek Realization, and he answered, "Who asks you to if you are satisfied with life as it is?" But he went on to explain that people often become dissatisfied with life and they turn to God for guidance. This insight explains why the good, comfortable, kind-hearted people seldom become seekers. They lack the spur of initial discontent to start them off. Christ said that those who seek shall find, but before one even knows that there is anything to seek, one may have to reject the sham satisfaction provided by everyday life. Tragic events may turn a nonseeker into a seeker, yet the call beckons the prosperous no less than the indigent, the successful as well as the failures. The call may stem from boredom, as well as tragedy.

There is also another, more psychological explanation why many egoists take the path (and it is only a matter of degree, because we are all egoists, more or less, until the ego is extinguished). Although committed to self-destruction, the ego has grand expectations of achievement. Some mystery religions have treated initiates like a king or a god for a year, only to be sacrificed at the year's end. This process symbolizes ego-death, except that on the spiritual path, we do not have a fixed term for our self-sacrifice, and we can postpone it indefinitely. Even if the ego chooses not to make the hazardous choice of self-denial, everyday life will confront it with the ultimate extinction of death.

The quest goes in alternate waves of expansion and contraction, symbolized by Jupiter and Saturn. Our task in this process remains quite simple—what we have to do is to keep the mind still, take cognizance of outer happenings, concentrate on the mere fact of Being, and remain poised and alert for promptings from within. It is as simple as that. Although it is simple, few people find it easy. While shaving or stirring the porridge, we are tempted to let the mind ramble on incessantly over "What I will say to George in the office?" and so on. These ramblings have two features in common. First, they center around a character called "I" who measures all events in terms of good and evil, advantage and disadvantage; sages declare this "I" to be fictitious. Second, these mental rumblings add nothing to the success of that presumptive character, but merely mull over what has already been decided or will have to be decided in due course. They have the disastrous effect of deafening the mind to the still, small voice of the Self and preventing spiritual intuition or awareness of Self from flowing. In this way the presumptive "I," like an evil ghost, seems to usurp clear awareness of the Self.

While the mind of the student is filled with rambling thought, the mind of the realized person is dead [to identification with thought]. Though this statement appears paradoxical, the mind of the Sage is quite alive for receiving impressions. Inwardly, it receives awareness and intuitions of the Self, while outwardly it cognizes things and events. In both cases, the mind does not usurp the role of creator, projecting an imaginary world for an illusory being. Still, receptive, able to reflect the light of the Self, the mind also functions more efficiently when set free from its habitual agitated state.

Most people find it rather difficult to end the mind's rumbling and to experience pure awareness of Being. Thus, the paths laid down by different religions offer them support. Asking oneself "Who am I?," being mindful of one's actions, watching the breath, repeating a mantra, concentrating on a scriptural text, or puzzling over an insoluble problem—all these are methods to control and still the mind.

As we begin to still the mind to a greater or lesser degree and for longer or shorter periods, we break through the barrier that blocks spiritual knowledge, and the awareness of our own Being begins to flood in. Sometimes it is pure and formless; other times it is garbed with bliss or ecstasy. Sometimes it is filled with healing grace or innate vigor; then, again, one may experience psychic or other extrasensory powers—all according to one's individual nature. In some people, the temporary stilling of the mind occurs with no striving or effort, and the barrier to experience falls away without their understanding of what is happening or why. These people are natural mystics.

With this understanding, we come back to the question of egoism and the alternate phases of expansion and contraction experienced during the quest. Each time the barrier is breached, the Water of Life flows through, although it might be only a slight trickle or a fitful jet. A feeling of expansion, grace, and well-being results, whether or not accompanied by any of the powers or experiences referred to above. But the lurking ego may quickly use these experiences for its own ends—for enjoyment, boasting, or glorification, all of which close the barrier and prepare us for a new period of contraction and aridity, which are common to most aspirants. And so the wheel goes round. It is necessary to always be alert, and when grace comes to avoid pilfering it or impeding its flow. Thus, when King Janaka attained realization, he said, "At last I have caught the thief (the ego) who has been robbing me all these years."

The ego has plenty of rewards to look forward to on the quest, rewards of a rarer and more exotic kind than it would find in the marketplace. There are ancient myths in which the hero has to pass by trees laden with jewels or rare fruits, but woe betide him if he stops to gather them. Warnings of dangers on the path are not fanciful; they are sober realities. Indeed, when the flow of grace is bounteous but the resistance of the ego is tenacious, the resultant stress may imbalance the mind. I have seen many such cases.

The most pernicious egoism occurs in the person who has already advanced far enough on the path to obtain certain experiences. The realized person is set free from ordinary rules of conduct and no longer needs them. In Old Testament language, such a person becomes "a law unto himself." Having direct apprehension of Divine Harmony and no egoistic impulses to act in opposition to it, the realized person needs no outer directives. This freedom has been recognized in various religions. For instance, the fourth-century Christian Desert Fathers, who were extreme in austerity, declared that one who had attained the goal could return to the cities of the world and live there unrecognized.

Based on real or alleged experiences, some individuals may claim to be above good and evil and feel free to indulge in various kinds of licentiousness. Such people are likely to corrupt themselves and others, especially when they set themselves up as gurus. The ego loves this form of indulgence, even though no such claim is valid. To those who claim to live above the law, only one valid benchmark exists: whether their ego has dissolved. Such people have no incentive to indulge in licentious behavior. Therefore, those who act licentiously in the name of a "higher law" are living proof that their egos still exist and that they are not authorized to act as self-realized sages. To do so would delude others, as well as themselves.

One conclusion is definite: The method or path an aspirant follows, in whatever religion, leads to the subsidence of the ego. Therefore, those who retain strong egoism (whether it manifests as arrogance, jealousy, licentiousness, avarice, or whatever else) remain very far from the goal, no matter what experiences they may enjoy. Whatever technique of inner purification they may follow, they must do the outer work of moral purification. While techniques differ in various paths, they all aim at the liquidation of the ego, a goal that can never be attained while egoism is harbored.

But why so many words? Living as a false individual self alienates one from the Universal Self or God and brings frustration. The intellectual argument that there is no individual self helps still less. To believe in the existence of a Supreme Self or God and consistently subordinate the interests of the presumptive individual self to the Supreme is a great help. However, the only way to complete fulfillment lies in the unwavering conviction pointed out in the *Bhagavad Gita* (2.16):

There is no existence of the unreal and no nonexistence of the Real.

"This" and "That"

Why should a quest be necessary? Why should a person not grow naturally into their true state, like a horse or an oak tree? Why should human beings alone, of all creatures, be tempted to misuse their faculties and have to curb their desires to grow to their true breadth and stature? To answer this question, we must understand what differentiates human beings from other creatures. Some researchers have attributed the difference simply to the greater intelligence and ability that comes from our more developed brain. This is patently untrue. Many creatures have greater ability than we do in one ability or another. A hawk has keener sight, a migratory bird has a better memory for places and directions, a dog has a stronger sense of smell, and a bat has a wider range of hearing. What really distinguishes human beings from other creatures is self-consciousness. Not only are we human beings, but we know consciously that we are. We may see this faculty with greater intelligence, but not in the commonly understood sense of outwardly turned intelligence. Being self-conscious implies the deliberate use of our faculties and the power of deciding how and whether to use them. And this power is also a necessity. Having the power to direct our faculties imposes on us the necessity of doing so, since even refusal to do so would be our choice or direction, and not spontaneous as with other creatures.

Theologians express the dilemma of human consciousness in the belief that God gave human beings free will. With it comes the choice of whether to obey or disobey God, and thus to work out our own weal or woe. Intellectuals often scoff at such doctrines, which are only picturesque expressions of fundamental truths. We simply cannot use our faculties as naturally as a bird or fox can, because we lack a natural human-action, while there is a natural bird-action or fox-action. Humans, of course, have certain natural instincts, just as a bird or fox has (i.e., the instincts to eat, procreate and preserve life), but humans may or may not choose to obey them in any specific situation related to the complexities of life. Our self-conscious existence forces us to choose how to use our faculties. Even when we attempt to use them in what is considered the natural way we are making a choice, and we could surely find someone to contest it. We call this choice free will, which is, therefore, not only a prerogative but an obligation for us.

Thus understood, free will has nothing to do with destiny. Free will is a power that we are compelled, by our own nature, to use, whether the use we make of it is predestined or not. If I have to decide whether to spend this evening at a dance, or in meditation, or whether to strike or forgive someone who has insulted me, the responsibility of deciding rests with me, whether the outcome is predetermined or not. If it is predetermined, my own past habit-forming and character-forming decisions in this and previous lifetimes have predetermined it. This decision, in its turn, will help to condition my mind, thus determining future decisions. In any case, since I do not know which of two decisions is predetermined, I have to choose one or the other.

However, it may be argued that deciding to use one's faculties does not imply the necessity of a spiritual quest. All people have to make decisions, whereas very few set forth on the quest. This is only too true. As the *Bhagavad Gita* (8.3) states, "Out of thousands, perhaps one seeks Realization." This quotation implies only the possibility, not the necessity, of the quest.

The quest brings the possibility of rising above the normal human state, but it involves also the possibility of falling below it. Thus, many Eastern scriptures warn so insistently that we must make good use of our human birth, because if we misuse this one, we may not attain another one so easily. Truly, no implacable outside power thrusts us lower down the scale if we misuse our human opportunities to rise higher. We owe our destiny to the impersonal law of cause and effect. We cannot blame a crow for greed, a cat for cruelty, a goat for lust. But human beings who allow themselves to be dominated by such qualities have voluntarily given them ascendancy over higher possibilities. If, in this way, they have forced their minds into a subhuman mold in this lifetime, they must expect their bodies to take the same mold in the next, since the body is only a reflection or condensation of the mind.

Naturally, not everyone who fails to take up the quest falls below the human state. There are many gradations within that state. There is the possibility of birth and death, occurring in an apparently endless and meaningless circle. Yet in the end, everyone has the freedom to rise above the human state or fall below it. And between each human death and rebirth there are heavens and hells to reap.

The quest does not mean simply a cultural interest in spirituality, such as taking in music or philosophy; it means a total dedication. It means making Realization the whole aim and purpose of life. And since eventual Realization is, by nature, the purpose of life, those who undertake the quest have understood life aright and live it purposefully, using it instead of being used by it.

Once embarked upon, the quest may assume a number of forms. It may appear primarily under the guise of getting or giving, but in fact both occur, for only by making oneself small enough to pass through the eye of a needle can one expand to infinity. On a *yogic* or *tantric* path, one develops latent powers beyond the awareness of the average person, but if the course is to succeed it demands the simultaneous surrender not only of the indulgence of desires, but of the desires themselves. On a devotional path, one craves perpetually to love, give, surrender, to be nothing in the hands of God, but power pours into this nothing, this self-effaced worshipper. For such a devotee, it is safer to concentrate on giving. By thus giving without seeking, one attains the kingdom of heaven. Christ said, "Attain first the kingdom of heaven and all else shall be added to you." If one seeks to attain all else first, the kingdom of heaven is not likely to be added.

Before we are drawn to the quest, we are directly conscious of only one being, which could therefore be called "this"—this which wants coffee for breakfast, this which has a toothache, this which decides to call on so-and-so or read such-and-such a book. We know other people, things, and events only indirectly, through our senses (including our reason, which *Vedanta* calls the "inner sense"). However, a time may come when we apprehend Being of another kind: potent, unconfined, awe-inspiring, which we may think of as "That." Hereafter, the dominant theme of life is the relationship between "this" and "That," between the individual who experiences, classifies, and decides and the dimly perceived Reality. Our mental training decides whether we regard "That" as other than "this" or as the hidden Self of it. In any case, theoretical conclusions help us very little. What opens before one is a dynamic venture, the attempt to subordinate "this" to "That." Ramana Maharshi said:

> Under whatever name and form one may worship the Absolute Reality, it is only a means for realizing it without name and form. That alone is true Realization, wherein one knows oneself in relation to that Reality, attains peace and realizes one's identity with It.
>
> —*Forty Verses on Reality* (v. 5)

The attempt to do this is the quest. Becoming convinced of the identity of "this" with "That" means realizing it. In fact, intellectual understanding arrives only as the preliminary position from which to set out on the quest of Realization. "This" feels not only the power, but also the grace and pervading beauty of "That," and is strongly attracted to it. Whether we call "That" God or Self, this is shaken by powerful waves of love and devotion toward it. The attraction is so powerful that "this" feels itself being drawn in to be devoured and merged in "That." It also senses that absorption will produce what is called "the peace that passeth all understanding." At the same time, "this" struggles against being absorbed, clinging tenaciously to the surface life which Christ exhorted it to give up. It still wants its own separate individual existence, along with its own decisions and enjoyments. Therefore, it may feel waves of resentment or actual hostility to "That."

> I sought to devour thee; come now and devour me; then there will be peace, Arunachala!
>
> —*The Marital Garland of Letters* (v. 28), by Sri Ramana Maharshi

That is why (except in the rarest of cases) the quest is not a single, simple event. Normally, "this" clings to its separate, individual life with one hand, while reaching out for the vast, universal life with the other. Moreover, the two cannot co-exist. "This" must surrender utterly to "That" and consent to be devoured before it can merge in the peace of supreme Identity. And it fights against it persistently and cunningly, constantly changing its ground, weapons, and tactics. When "this" is dislodged from one fortress, it slips around the rear of the attacker and sets up another.

Therefore, the uneven course that the quest takes is never a gradual, smooth ascent. It always goes in alternate waves of grace and deprivation, expansion and contraction. A phase when life is a lilt of beauty is followed by one of harsh aridity, when all that was achieved seems lost, and all grace withdrawn. This alternation happens because when "this" turns in love and humility to "That," it draws upon itself the grace, which is uninterruptedly radiating from "That," like light from the sun; "this" then steals the grace for its own use or aggrandizement. Whether in thought or deed, it grows proud, considers the grace its own, and thus interposes its own dark shadow before the luminosity of "That," causing an eclipse and shutting off the flow of grace. Again and again it repeats this pattern, learning only gradually and by repeated bitter experience. Only when, in final desperation, it brings itself to complete surrender, does lasting peace appear. Then "That" becomes "This." There is no other.

Self and Ego

With practice, you can rest in Being, just as you now breathe or eat. And, as with breathing or eating, there is no need to think about it before consciously experiencing it. Both a stone and a person can "be" unconsciously. The difference is that a person can *consciously* "be."

When you feel this sense of Being, this pure "I-am," you find that it does not fall into any category. It is neither yours nor is it not yours; it is neither divided from other people nor united with them; it just *is*. And it is pure, simple consciousness. You cannot say that you are conscious of it, because there is no separate you to be conscious of it. You are it and it is you.

Additionally, the experience is a very blissful one, free from worry and sorrow. You recollect this only when looking back at it, because while it lasts you do not bother about such questions. In fact, upon looking back, you realize that while it lasted you were not thinking at all but just seeing, hearing, and cognizing, without the experience intruding upon you and without being disturbed by it at all.

Normally, you experience yourself as an individual being, separate from all others, liking some things and people and disliking others. You do not need to work at this because people usually feel this way normally.

You do not have two different selves, but rather two ways of experiencing Being. One leads to serenity and happiness; the other leads to anger, jealousy, frustration and all manner of suffering. To deal with this dilemma, some religions teach rejection of the ego. Thus, Christ said that those who give up their life for His sake (for the Spirit or Self) will find it (the Self), while those who seek to save their life will lose it. Other religions teach that there is not really an ego at all (as in the Buddhist doctrine of *anatta*). These two positions make no difference to a spiritual aspirant because whether the ego exists or not, it *appears* to exist; this "apparent self" has to be seen for what it really is.

Most people live simply as the ego, not knowing any other possibility. How did this state come about? According to psychology, the very young child has no ego-sense. Western spiritual tradition also holds that our earliest ancestors also had no ego-sense. The rise of the ego brought about the differentiation of good and evil, which led to the "fall" of humanity from the ego-free state called "paradise" and to the present ego-ridden state of our strife-filled world.

A human being comes into the world with various faculties, including the mental faculty. Very early in life, this mental faculty begins to find some of the reports made by the other faculties pleasant and others unpleasant. It then builds itself up into a fictitious person who constantly demands the pleasant experiences and rejects or tries to reject the unpleasant ones. This fictitious person, which we call "the mind," is the same as the ego. When Maharshi or any other spiritual master says that the mind of the realized person is "dead," it does not mean that the mental faculty is in any way impaired. If Bhagavan looks at a calendar, he can tell the date like anyone else. The mind of the realized sage no longer functions as ruler of the other faculties and indeed of life itself—planning the future, regretting the past, hoping, fearing, or feeling pride.

All spiritual teaching guides and encourages us to seek liberation from the ego and realization of the Self. The two are the same. To say "There is no ego," "The ego is an illusion," or that "The Self already is," does not in any way free us from the obligation of realizing the Self. Every time we act selfishly in thought, word, or deed, we receive ample motivation to seek liberation from the illusion of ego. We accomplish nothing when we say there is no ego yet behave as though there were, because actions speak louder than words. Living as though there were an ego prevents us from realizing that there is not. It also prevents gaining liberation from it.

The question may arise, "If I like the ego-state, why shouldn't I be left at peace in it?" The answer is, "You don't like it." Nobody does, because the ego itself (or the illusion of one) does not leave us at peace. In describing one of humanity's greatest afflictions, Solomon listed "a servant when he ruleth." The mental faculty is perfectly equipped to be a servant, but the mind makes itself a ruler. It is insatiable. However favorable one's circumstances, it always craves more—more pleasure, more admiration, more success. At the same time, it is eternally insecure, vulnerable to sickness, bereavement, old age, destitution, and, ultimately and unavoidably, to death. Yet plagued by this ego-self—frustrated, insecure, and even driven to consider death as an escape from it—few people have the clear understanding and the determination to give it up! That is the perpetual mystery.

The next question may arise, "How do I know that I'll be better off, less frustrated, and more content if I reject the ego?" As Bhagavan says, "Who asks the question?" Being ego-free is the natural state, what I am innately. It is also the carefree and deathless state. One feels intuitively that it is so, and if empirical evidence also were needed, we can find it in the lives of the liberated. A sage lives immersed in bliss, whether or not the apparent circumstances of life seem favorable. What sage has ever complained?

But some will ask, "Are there also positive gains?" Who for? The faculties, set free from the tyrant mind, are able to grow naturally, no longer warped, stunted, or shut off from the sunlight. Moreover, the mind, the usurper, gloats at the prospect of the gains that will accrue as a reward for its fictitious death and asks if there are positive gains! This tactic represents one of the mind's strongest lines of defense and counterattack.

Then if we decide to abjure the seeming-self for the true Self, the question remains: How do we do it?

As a useful introduction, we need to keep in mind the reality of the Self and the unreality of the seeming self, the ego. What we understand on a mental level can never be more than an introduction, although a useful one. Sri Krishna gave it to Arjuna first before speaking about the discipline of life his charioteer was to follow.

After acquiring an intellectual understanding, we then adopt a discipline of life. Such a discipline might entail living each day as it comes based on the assumed unreality of the individual self. Living this way implies cool, efficient, impersonal activity such as Sri Krishna enjoins in the *Bhagavad Gita*, doing what is right because it is right, not for profit or pleasure. It does not follow, however, that there must be no profit or pleasure in life. Merchants naturally sell at a profit because that is how they make their living; a married man naturally expects pleasure from his family life. In these cases, profit and pleasure should not override duty and become the dominating motives in life.

However, even a life of disinterested activity cannot normally dissolve the ego-sense. Such an approach usually needs to be reinforced by a stronger and more forceful campaign, involving either surrender or inquiry. Sri Krishna in the *Gita* enjoins surrender; Vasishta in the *Yoga Vasishta* enjoins Self-inquiry. When asked about this subject, Maharshi said: "There are two ways; ask yourself 'Who am I?' or surrender." The mind, which acts as though it were the ruler and owner of the faculties, must abdicate and surrender them and itself to pure Being, the Self. Alternatively, it should look inward and perceive the true nature of the Self, or Being.

Lines from "A Testament"

Just as a nighttime dream seems real enough,
So long it lasts, within your mortal mind,
So your life's journey, whether smooth or
rough—
Between deep hedgerows fragrantly entwined
With honeysuckle, all the air athrob
With singing of the birds, your steps combined
With those of loved companion, such as rob
Exhaustion of its pain, night of its fears,
Or over arid crags, where not to sob
For weariness were hard when the sun sears
And only thorn-trees cast a stunted shade,
While all ahead the naked shale appears—
All that same dream-stuff out of which is made
Your mortal self. All that is known or seen.
With you in it, a pageant is, displayed
Harmless in you, like pictures on a screen.
Awake! for dawn has set the sky aflame!
Awake from dreaming what has never been
To find the universe entire a game
Forever, new, you evermore the same.

Frustration and Fulfillment

Normally, one feels an individual selfhood; that is, one feels and reacts as an ego. However, one can have an intuition of pure Being without identifying as an individual. So long as one believes in the reality of the ego, pure Being will appear as "other" and be called "God," because it is indeed other than the ego. When one feels or perceives the ego to be unreal, one will feel pure Being as real and call it the "Self." The question is not whether there is a God apart from you, but whether there is a "you" apart from God.

The question for each person is whether one regards oneself as a real, separate being. If one does, one sets up an image of that being. However, that image is imaginary, as the term implies, and because it is unreal, it cannot endure. When the imagined self confronts Reality, which is one of the names of God, it is broken down in the divine encounter. Actually, Reality does not break it down; the false self, the ego, breaks itself by asserting its imagined Reality. When we assert an apparent separate will against the inevitability of Reality, we become frustrated. As Bhagavan said when we add "Thy Will be done" to a prayer, we should remember that it will be done anyway, whether we say so or not. The Divine Will, which is the essential harmony, will automatically take place.

Pure Being, operating through each seeming individual's faculties and tendencies, is shaping them towards perfection. As Christ said, "Be ye perfect, as your Father which is in Heaven is perfect." However, because the unreal image of itself, which the ego molds, does not agree with the divine likeness of the perfected self, it has to be broken down and recognized for what it is. The more our self-image diverges from the true pattern of being "made in the likeness of God," the more we become disillusioned and frustrated and tend to become embittered against fate. In the quaint language of the New Testament, Christ called this "kicking against the pricks." On the other hand, the more we accept the truth of our real nature, the more grace and blessing we find in life. This acceptance does not need to be conscious and philosophically conversant; it may be a silent humility, submitting unquestioningly to the subtle intuition of clarity.

The perfect fulfillment of an individual's wishes comes when one has ceased to have any wishes. That is to say, it comes when one has ceased to have any self-will in opposition to the

Universal Will. Even on the dualistic level of worshipper and Worshipped, some saints have declared that God has such love for them as to grant whatever they ask for. But if one studies the lives of such people, one finds that nothing they asked for was egoistic in nature. One may even find that this overwhelming feeling of Divine Benevolence was not inconsistent with poverty, sickness, or imprisonment. It simply never occurred to them to plead against such things. Since there is no longer any opposition against the flow of Universal Being manifesting through the "individual" faculties, the Divine does not have to break down or humble the "apparent" self.

Once, a group of devotees were speaking to Bhagavan about a shortage of funds at the Ashram, and he said, "If I gave a single thought to the need for money, so much would come in that you could not count it." During Maharshi's last illness, Sri Viswanathan (a senior devotee of Bhagavan) said, "If Bhagavan would give just one thought to getting better the sickness would end." To this, the Master replied in a tone of disgust, "Who could have such a thought?" He meant, "Who could have self-will to oppose the Divine Will in the flow of events?" Even in the smallest things (and it was only in the smallest things that anything approaching a wish could be discerned), Bhagavan found immediate fulfillment. If he picked up a book to refer to some passage, it would normally open to the very page he needed.

He once remarked to an attendant that he needed a notebook, and K. K. Nambiar (a devotee of Sri Ramana, who lived in the nearby city of Madras) dreamed that Maharshi needed one and brought one the next morning. Bhagavan happened to mention oranges at the Ashram, and someone sent a crate of them next day. In general, he did not express wishes; he had none to express.

Those who have abandoned the ego have escaped frustration. They feel the worthlessness of the ego, and at the same time, whether it is a paradox or not, the Divine Benevolence and fulfillment it has brought them.

Who Is "Who"?

We ask, "Who am I?" but is there an "I"? Initially, we presume that there is. Then, we ask who or what it is. There just IS—not I, he, it, or anything, just IS. We try to divide up this simple IS by pronouns—I, he, you—and by "this" and "that," but is it really divisible? I feel Being and use the word "I" for it, but that does not mean that there is any separateness about it. You also feel Being and use the same word "I" for it of course, because it is the same being.

Outwardly, Being takes form as a world of things and events. It cognizes this world by means of "my" faculties. In fact, everyone has this sense of "me" and "my." Being has three aspects. First, there just Is. Second, there is the manifest world. Third (or perhaps this should be put second), there is the focal point, the cluster of faculties called "me," through which the manifest world is cognized. In all cases, pure Being or Is-ness remains the same, whether the manifest world and the "me" are there or not.

People often remark, "I am an infinitesimal, evanescent fragment in this vast universe." True, but it is no less true that this vast universe is an infinitesimal, evanescent appearance within me. What-is remains the same, whether manifested in the universe or not. The pure sense of Being that I feel just is; it is the same as what-is. Saying that there is no "I" is the same as saying that there is nothing else.

To say that there is a subjective "me" and an objective "me" would open the door to misunderstanding, because all technical terms do that. However, at the same time it might point the way to understanding. Technical terms do that, too; that is why we find it so hard to abandon them. We could see the subjective "me" as the focal point between Being and the manifest world, and the objective "me" as that part of the manifest world which expresses itself on a par with you, Susan, James, and John. When, true to its nature, the subjective me sees every objective me equally; that is to say, it loves its neighbor as itself. It is attracted exclusively and completely back toward Being. That is to say, it loves God with all its heart and mind and strength.

In fact, fallen humanity is not true to its nature. People need authentic meditation experience before they even begin to feel impersonal "I"-ness, the unity of Being. Even when they do, they often continue feeling the restricted individual "I"-

sense. Every time I feel a thrill of pleasure at being praised or annoyance at being criticized; if I take the corner seat in a train and leave my companion a less comfortable place; when I take a second cup of tea and there is not enough to go round; or imagine myself in some role or dread some eventuality, I am proclaiming the individual "me" in action. And actions speak louder than words. What good is it to say that there is no ego, yet behave as though there were? Obversely, living on the assumption that there is an ego prevents one from realizing that there is not, and from realizing our true nature.

Many great Teachers, including Ramana Maharshi, have said that we are not bound, so there can be no Liberation. Yet, paradoxically, they have also urged us to seek Liberation. We must have a clear understanding of the words we use to avoid being tangled up in them. What are we liberated from? From the ego, our belief in an ego, or the illusion of an ego? If there is no ego then, of course, there can be no bondage to it and no need for Liberation from it. But so long as I live as though there were an ego, and take offense at an insult, there is an ego for me, and I am bound by it or by the service I render to it.

While my true Self is not bound, bondage to the (real or illusory) ego obscures the true Self. Realization of the Self is the same as Liberation from the ego.

What does it matter if I believe in a separate, individual self, an ego? Why do spiritual teachers speak of it as a sort of crime? Because it is. It is "original sin." All technical terms, such as Self, ego, sin, God, or mind mislead us. These terms, which become personified like characters on a stage, need to be reexamined from time to time. Being (what-is) uses the mental faculty to report and circulate perceptions from the manifest world as submitted by my other faculties. However, very early in life this mental faculty begins to find some of the reports made to it pleasant and others disturbing. In this way, the mental faculty builds itself up into a fictitious person who demands the pleasant experiences and rejects (or tries to reject) the unpleasant ones. For this purpose, it uses and disposes of the other faculties. We call this fictitious person "mind" or "ego." They are the same.

Me and the World

What do I know about myself and the world? Directly, apart from what I read and am told, I know that I have certain senses—seeing, hearing, touch, taste, and smell—which report a body and a world outside it. I also have a mental faculty to which the senses report.

Taking into account what I read and what I am told, I know also that their report is fallacious and that this outer world is illusory and has only the reality that my perceptions mistakenly give it. Sages have always told us this; now physical science does, too. If I see a hard, red ball, I know that its redness is just the way that my optical apparatus reports vibrations of a certain frequency. If there is a bang when I hit it with a piece of wood, my ears report a vibration of another frequency. Similarly, I endow it with roundness and hardness. In reality (so far as there is a physical reality), the red ball is just a cluster of atoms dashing about in empty space, by far the greater part of each single atom being, itself, empty space.

Furthermore, both sages and scientists assure us that the whole, endless variety of things is reducible to uniformity—call it *prakriti*, or an energy-field.

Let us return to the observation of myself. My mind not only receives reports from the senses but also passes judgment on them, dividing them into pleasant and unpleasant, desirable and undesirable. It develops an urge to seek the former and avoid the latter. For instance, I find the smell of a rose pleasant, that of garlic unpleasant, and therefore I have an impulse to put a bowl of roses in the living room and shut the garlic up in an airtight tin. And I know that these reactions are mental because when I am asleep or under hypnosis, I do not experience them.

I spoke of a mental faculty to which the senses make their fallacious reports, but what we call the mind is much more than that. It is an intelligence that looks upon itself as an individual being. It possesses senses and uses them to acquire what it likes and avoid what it dislikes, thus becoming immersed in a turbulent sea of ambitions, hopes, fears, desires, and regrets. This individual being that it imagines itself to be is just as illusory as the apparent world of solid objects that the senses report exists outside itself. When we say that the mind of a *Jnani* is "dead," it does not mean that he has no mental faculty. If he looks at a clock, he can tell what time it is. In every way, his mental faculty functions as well as anyone else's—in fact even better, since it is unobstructed by the interests of an imaginary person.

Spirituality has devised various techniques for exposing this imaginary identity that we call "mind," or "ego." Aspirants may deny what the mind craves, habituate it to what it dislikes, shut off the senses, and refuse to listen to their fallacious reports. They may focus attention on Universal Being, invoke it, bow down to it, act according to duty, and accept whatever comes. One can also try to expose this imaginary self in a direct manner by remaining alert and watchful but refusing to give directions to the senses, by stepping off the throne one has usurped, and by refusing to let the mind be more than a mental faculty.

It may be that we cannot do this immediately, completely, and continually; but gradually, and for increasing periods, we can. We will feel a peculiar vibration, a sense of aliveness in both body and mind, a sense of rightness and of divine content (which is a far higher state than divine discontent. Discontent with the false is an impetus to seek the true; contentment derives its basis from recognition of the true).

Perhaps one finds various powers and perceptions developing as the senses and faculties are freed from the stunting grip of the ego-mind. Then—and there is no perhaps about this—one finds the ego-mind slipping back into the driver's seat and trying to take control of these senses and faculties, use them, and enjoy them. In this way, they are lost or spoiled. This kind of setback occurs as part of the cyclic nature of the path, which alternates between expansion and contraction. Constant alertness is needed. "Eternal vigilance is the price of freedom." The freedom we seek is from the ego-mind.

When the ego-mind is held in abeyance, powers flow through—different powers with different people, according to their nature. But wanting them means the ego-mind is back again, which then impedes them, spoils them, or makes them harmful to oneself and others. Christ said, "Of my own self I can do nothing."

The spiritual seeker must keep up this aloofness from the mind until it is not only in abeyance, but is extinguished. But will that happen? Who asks that? Who doubts that it will? The ego-mind will, the arch-hypocrite piously doubting its own death-sentence. Let it only be still. That is all that is required of it. Universal Power will flow as long as it is not obstructed. Maharshi said, "Submit to me and I will strike down the mind." Whether one calls the power "God," "Self," "Christ," "Krishna," or "Bhagavan," one has only to surrender and stop interfering, planning, and directing its course.

Sometimes a person has an experience of pure Being. One just "is" and feels the fact of Being. Only later, he or she may appreciate that this is pure consciousness. Thoughts can be suspended, but even when they occur, they do not interrupt the flow of consciousness. However, it is not necessarily blissful; it is not *Satchitananda*—Being-Consciousness-Bliss. One may feel disappointed, along with the belief that something must be wrong with either the teaching or oneself. But, no; it is merely a case of the mind eavesdropping. "Who" feels no bliss? I do not. But that "I" has no business being there at all. One is a mortal spying on the gods. Being not only feels bliss but *is* bliss. Only the absence of the reporter "I" is a necessary condition for this revelation.

Concentration and Detachment

What we need is simply to take things as they come, reacting in the way we feel to be right, interfering as little as possible. Then things will happen correctly of their own accord, and grace will flow unimpeded. We do not have to induce divine grace to flow, only to refrain from obstructing it.

Two kinds of obstruction prevent grace from flowing and make the path long and arduous: distraction and attachment. Therefore, we have to cultivate their opposites: concentration and detachment.

Let us first consider concentration. The untrained mind

seldom can concentrate steadily on a particular thought at all for any length of time. It flits about restlessly from thought to thought. The same phenomenon occurs in conversation. For instance, at a social gathering people seldom talk things through to a conclusion or discuss any subject seriously, but instead butterfly talk, flitting from one topic to another. Let the person with an untrained mind see how long the mind can be held to any one theme. Getting past thirty seconds would be a great achievement for such a person. How much training, then, do we need to hold the mind to pure awareness?

Some teachers prescribe exercises for concentration, but this approach is seldom more than a parlor game. When it does have any effect, it may do more harm than good unless the mind is simultaneously being purified. Egoism is more dangerous in a concentrated mind than in a distracted one.

The mind automatically gets both strengthened and purified by turning to prayer, recitation, or meditation on (or the experience of) pure Being. The aspirant needs practice, which may be difficult at first. On the other hand, practice may release a flow of grace far in excess of what personal effort seems to merit. Unusual skills or powers may come to those who have already developed the power of concentration, even though their fields are unrelated to spirituality, such as to chess players, scientists, artists, or even criminals. One who has openly used the power of concentration in a malicious manner may, when induced to turn it aright, make equally spectacular progress. There are a number of famous examples of this. The Sage Valmiki, author of the *Ramayana*, was a murderer and robber until a sudden revulsion turned him in the right direction. The same thing happened to one of the great *Marathi* poet-saints of medieval India. Buddha went out into the forest to seek Angulimala, a notorious killer and plunderer, conquered him by the spiritual power flowing through him, and brought him back as a yellow-robed monk. People tell similar stories about St. John the Evangelist on the Island of Patmos, and St. Francis of Assisi. In these cases, in turning against the ego by a tremendous act of will, they overcame their ruthlessness by concentrating the mind and enabling divine grace to flow through them.

If lack of concentration destroys one's ability to maintain steady self-awareness, lack of detachment destroys one's will to do the same. We need to be detached and concentrated at the same time. Said differently, we need true humility, a quality which is not in essence comparative at all. When we are humble, we do not compare ourselves unfavorably with others (which may involve a good dose of hypocrisy), but we appear in utter poverty and submission before the Supreme. To avoid this exposure, the ego throws out tentacles; clutches at possessions, enjoyment, status, and power; and puts up a fight.

The qualities which religion denounces as "sins" are in fact those which inflate the ego and prevent its total submission. Whether one speaks in terms of duality or Oneness, whether one calls That "God" or "Self," the fact remains that the ego must be deflated enough to pass through the eye of a needle before it can return to That. Ethical philosophers who have tried to clarify the nature of sin, explain that our conception of it arises from social convenience, and condemn only those actions that harm society. They are quite wrong. Sins are modes of action, which primarily harm oneself by inflating the ego and making it unwilling to yield.

The ego has its roots in attachments and survives through them. The ego cannot renounce the world inwardly as long as it clings to it through attachments. The ego and its attachments are mutually dependent: the ego cannot be destroyed so long as there are attachments, and attachments cannot be destroyed so long as there is an ego. The "holy war" can take the form of attacking attachments to starve out the ego, or attacking the ego so that with its death the attachments also perish. Actually, we are to carry on both types of campaigns simultaneously, since neither by itself is a passport to success; both require courage and perseverance, along with skill and alertness because the ego is very cunning. Deprived of one outlet, it will switch its attention to another. Deprived of a gross outlet, it will find a subtle one. When vigilance is relaxed over captured strongholds the ego will return there, so that one can never count on demolishing attachments one by one. Mythological tales symbolize the ego's ability to assume a new form when the old one is threatened by the hero's combat with an enemy that constantly changes form. The hero has to be equally alert and change with it—into an eagle when it becomes a bird, into a lion when it becomes a beast, and so on. These stories symbolize the constant springing of attachments as combat with a giant or monster that grows two new heads for each one that is cut off. To vanquish the monster, the hero must strike directly at its heart.

Bhagavan recommended an opposite approach in striking at the ego. Naturally, we give no scope to attachments. We keep them in check and surrender them as far as possible, but we attack the ego directly. Bhagavan compared the ego to a tree and its attachments to the branches. If you cut off branches, it continues to put out new ones; Self-inquiry is an attempt to uproot the tree itself. As I have said, there is no easy recipe for success; the quest is a path for heroes. Additionally, as in warfare, heroes must be wise, as well as brave, using their forces to the best advantage. Attacking the ego directly through Self-inquiry affords the most direct approach. But it must be a real attack. Intellectual understanding that the ego is unreal does little to weaken its propensities. Otherwise, it continues to be nourished and holds us back from the bliss of realized Identity. Attachments have a strong, emotional force and can be removed only by a stronger force. Love and devotion often supply this power. Someone who, on the basis of doctrinal understanding, criticizes a *bhakta,* a divine lover, is like one who sits at the foot of a mountain with a good map in hand and disapproves of a climber, saying, "That fellow will never reach the top; his map only goes three quarters of the way up." Perhaps so; but maybe the *bhakta,* when reaching that point, will see the way clearly with no need for any further map. In any case, the divine lover is already above the heat and haze of the plains, while the critic may be no better off with an unused map.

Love—and it must be real love—can destroy attachments. That is the test. Some have asked how one is to love God. Some, in the name of spirituality, recommend that "we count His blessings on us, while thinking of all our sins and His forgiveness," but this is quite phony. Even humanly, one does not love out of gratitude. Such a mentality presumes two persons, God and ego. But, if God is all-powerful and we as individual egos love Him out of gratitude for caring for our wants, we can equally blame Him for not caring for them, for sending sickness, privation, bereavement, and, ultimately, death. This is a completely erroneous attitude. The individual is, by nature, drawn to that which is Universal; it only has to stay still and forget its desires and interests. Then the individual will feel the natural power of divine attraction, which is love; the individual also feels attachment, but if the divine attraction is powerful enough, it can overcome the attachment.

The two methods of knowledge and devotion may seem mutually exclusive in theory, but in practice they are not. One can seek the inner guru while at the same time revering the outer guru. We should use whatever tool proves most effective.

Faith

Faith means much more than belief. Buddha, for instance, disapproved of belief, preferring that his followers try out every principle for themselves. Yet, he insisted strongly on the need for *shraddha* (faith). Faith also does not mean the conviction that what one wants will come about or that prayers will be granted. Take again the example of Buddha: he did not teach belief in a God who answers prayers. What, then, was the faith he spoke of, and in whom or what?

We face life with a feeling of our own individual existence. We also have an intuition of pure Being, perhaps a fleeting recollection of complete certitude. Faith means surrender to and trust in this pure Being, whether we consider it apart from ourselves or our very essence. Ultimately, faith means abnegation of the individual being or ego.

It does not necessarily mean the conviction that one's prayers will be answered. It means acceptance of the unimportance or even unreality of the individual who prays, or at any rate, its complete subordination to That to which it prays. This subordination results in removal of the obstructions to the free flow of the Divine Harmony. In other words, it leads to an attitude of "Thy Will be done," whether expressed verbally or not. Additionally, since Divine Harmony is what is right and necessary, such an attitude does in fact bring about the answering of prayers, especially of unasked prayers, since even the asking is an intrusion of self-will. There is a beautiful little book called *The Son Liveth*, by Frank Drake, which begins with a father praying for his son's recovery from severe illness and develops into both father and son accepting whatever may come.

This is not a supine attitude. On the contrary, there is great power in it, far more than in the conscious mind. Spiritual teachers declare the power of such faith. Power flows naturally; only the conscious mind shuts it off. What is needed is submission without interference. Therefore, it is necessary to admit one's inability to use it and surrender in complete faith to That Power. Thus, indirectly, we remove the obstruction to its beneficent flow.

Sri Bhagavan says that if one is firm in the belief that a Higher Power guides us, there need not be any concern about what happens. Then, as doubts are cleared away, the devotee remains perfectly happy in that faith.

The faith of each is in accordance with his nature, O Bharata. Man is made up of his faith; as a man's faith is, so is he.
—*Bhagavad Gita* (17.3)

Good and Evil

Christ said that evil must come. Why? Christ was God incarnate and God is omnipotent. Then why must evil come? Could not God will it not to come?

Christ did not stop there. He added, "But woe unto him through whom it cometh." Again, why? If evil must come, why should the person who is instrumental in bringing it be condemned? Is it not unjust?

Since there is a deceptive simplicity in these sayings, we must probe deeper. In order to do so, we also must ask why Adam and Eve were free from the knowledge of good and evil in their Edenic state, and why its acquisition caused their exile from paradise and fall into a state of toil and suffering.

The whole universe outflows from the pure, formless Being of God into an increasingly condensed form of devolution, then returns through ever-rarified spheres to union with the Formless (evolution). Physically, the undifferentiated basic substance or energy coalesces into atoms, which are a miniature solar system. These atoms pin together into molecules, then substances, primitive organisms, and gradually into increasingly elaborate beings. Spiritually, as beings evolve in complexity their consciousness is limited by their physical and mental vehicles (called "sheaths" in *Vedanta*). Is the creation of Adam and his union with Eve the point at which the devolving human consciousness meets and fuses with a physical body evolved to the point of being a fit vehicle for a soul? Does Eve symbolize the physical form that, from one point of view, completes human beings and from another point of view limits them?

Suppose, at this point of fusion of soul and body, one lived in a state of harmony without self-will and egoism. Without denying one's true nature or asserting one's independence from God, one would live in the pristine beauty of the world without introducing corruption into nature or oneself. Indeed, one would be in paradise. Human beings would be living in what anthropologists call the food-gathering stage. However, anthropologists do not understand that since the outer world reflects one's inner consciousness, the world would be more bounteous, the land more fertile, and the weather more clement. The so-called "primitive" tribes that eke out a precarious existence today as food-gatherers no more compare with this happy childhood of humanity than the retarded mind knows the happiness of real childhood.

In such a paradise, there would be no "good" because there would be no "evil" with which to compare it. Everything would be good in a different sense, in the sense of being right, as it should be, true to its own nature. As the Bible says, "And God saw everything that he had made, and behold, it was very good."

Our perceptions get entangled into self-will when we regard ourselves as separate beings independent from the Universal Being of God. We then meet the serpent, the ego, the adversary who tempts us through the body—that is, through Eve. Some things now seem desirable or "good" to us, while others seem undesirable or "evil." We then "fall" into craving and fear, a condition that exiles us from the paradise of our spontaneous, carefree state and makes us subject to death. Our pure consciousness does not die; it returns to union with God. Only the ego, the self-will, has to die. Under the lash of fear and desire, life becomes hazardous; needs increase, demanding toil, accumulation; and enmity arises. Hereafter, although humanity pursues its outward course into ever-greater spiritual darkness and alienation, the life of each intelligent person is, or should be, a struggle to return to that lost paradise. The journey of return reverses the poles and values by which we live. What we once found desirable becomes "evil," since it leads away from good into ego-assertion. What we used to find undesirable becomes "good," since it leads through mortification of the ego to union with God. Life is a war between good and evil, and we have to choose one side or the other.

How do these points throw light on Christ's saying that evil must come? Creation is not an act that happened once and for all; it is continuous. Strangely enough, even scientists have come to this understanding. The outgoing from Oneness into form and the return from diversity to union is the nature of continuous creation. One might even say that this movement defines creation. Therefore, as long as there is creation, as long as there is a universe, this movement must continue. If it stopped, the universe would stop. However, on the human plane the outgoing involves an alienation from God into ego-assertion and is therefore "evil," while the incoming involves a return to conscious union with God and is therefore "good." In other words, the outgoing movement into self-will or ego-assertion represents one-half of the process of human creation. If there were no outgoing into manifestation, there could be no return—that is to say, no creation, no universe. To say that there could be a coming back without a going out is nonsense. Applied to the human level, this means that there could be no alienation from God on condition that there was no return to God, and no evil on condition that there was no good (but then there would be no human beings).

Theologians of an earlier day asserted that humanity had to fall through Adam in order to be redeemed by Christ. Some modern critics have derided this view and called it crude, but truly their understanding of it is crude. Rightly understood, this understanding is profound: There must be an outgoing from God before there can be a conscious return to union with the Source. In the life of each separate individual, also, the self-will, the ego, must be developed so that there can be return through grace to union.

Then what about the second part of Christ's saying: "But woe unto him through whom it cometh?" There is nothing arbitrary or unjust about this statement according to spiritual law (rightly understood, theological truths are natural laws).

The perfect saint who has laid down his life for Christ's sake can say with St. Paul, "I live, yet not I but Christ in me." Everyone else has both tendencies at work—alienation and ego-assertion, along with return and ego-dissolution. In all except the pure saint or complete villain both forces are actually working, however feeble and fitful one or the other may be. Given the wide spectrum of human development, these two forces are balanced differently in people's lives. This variety accounts for life's infinite richness.

The alienating tendency puts one in the grip of a disruptive inner force that takes the form of grasping, cruelty, arrogance, and other destructive forces. The alienating tendency spreads evil in the world but also, in doing so, creates an attraction towards evil in people, leaving them defenseless against these forces. Christ's saying does not imply that someone will punish evildoers (though the chain reaction they set up may well result in that), but observes that they put themselves at the mercy of destructive forces. People do not sin without an incentive. Ultimately, any incentive that is based on false values makes things appear desirable (which would not be so to a truly harmonious mind) and incites people to inharmonious activity. Such activity has a profound effect on people's character and affects their destiny.

Effort, Grace, and Destiny

It is said that an aspirant must make effort on the path, but that grace is also necessary and that in the end Realization is bestowed by grace, not achieved by effort. According to the *Upanishad,* the *Atman* chooses whom it will.

This is a complex saying. Those with a powerful spiritual urge are not concerned about it, since they strive by nature, drawn to the quest without any thought of reward. Those, however, with very active minds and less than ardent spirits might puzzle over this saying. They might ask why should any effort be made at all if the final achievement is bestowed not by effort but by grace. They may also ask why the *Atman* should choose one person rather than another. For questions like these, I will try to clarify the saying.

Who is the "you" that has to make effort, and who is the "God" or "*Atma*" that chooses and that bestows grace on one person rather than another?

The essence of a person is pure Spirit, pure Being, or pure Universal Consciousness. This Spirit endures in the stone, blossoms in the tree, prowls in the lion; but only in human beings does it live and knows it lives. The difference between human beings and other animals is not that we have greater ability than animals (in many ways we have less), but that we know consciously that we are human beings. When the human mind looks outward, it dominates the world. When it looks inward, it knows and reflects Being as the Essence and Source of the world. However, the ability to turn one's gaze inward also implies the ability not to do so, to regard oneself as a completely autonomous individual and to forget the inner Reality.

Different religions express this simple truth through myth, allegory, and doctrine that people might find puzzling, asserting that God gave us free will, which implies the freedom to rebel. Christianity teaches that human beings have fallen because of original sin. The Book of Genesis tells the story of how humanity fell into the domain of opposites, the realm of good and evil. All these allegories state the simple truth that the ego can either look inward to its source or outward to the world of multiplicity and separation.

The mind creates the ego, a seemingly complete, autonomous individual self which, although illusory, seems to be real. Hinduism calls this state *ajnana,* or ignorance, while Christianity calls it "Original Sin." Islam refers to this state as *kufr,* or "denial."

This primal ignorance of our nature obstructs Self-realization and must be removed. Yet, masters say that Self-realization is not something new to be achieved, but an eternally existent state to be discovered or revealed. They compare it to an overcast sky: the clear sky does not have to be created; only the clouds covering it need to be blown away. They also compare Self-realization to a pond overgrown with waterlilies: the water, which is there all the time, can be revealed by clearing away the plants that have overgrown it.

The rediscovery of our true nature constitutes the effort which spiritual teachers and scriptures describe. The mind has created the obstruction; the mind has to remove it. However, merely to recognize that the ego is illusory (as nondualists teach) or that the ego must surrender to the Spirit that created it (as dualists maintain) is far from constituting the full effort required.

The effort involves the will and emotions, as well as the understanding, and, therefore, it has to be persistent, determined, and skillful. The ego has put out tentacles that cling to the world, and either these have to be lopped off or the ego itself, eradicated. Because the ego craves the admiration or submission of other egos, religions therefore enjoin humility. Because the ego craves enjoying and taking credit for what it creates rather than acting as a mere channel through which Spirit works, religions sometimes prescribe celibacy and asceticism and always recommend against self-indulgence. While masters in different religions prescribe various ways of conducting the fight, the goal in every case remains the same: the taming or destruction of the ego, along with the discovery that it never really existed.

The methods that I have been alluding to consist mainly in curtailing the ego's outer manifestations and causing the mind to turn inward to the Self or Spirit behind it. One also can proceed in the opposite direction by turning inward to the Spirit and deriving enough strength to renounce the outer manifestations. This is the path of love and devotion, which involves worshipping God, surrendering to Him, calling upon His Name, and striving to serve and remember Him with one's whole life. Aspirants can follow either path or both together. A third path also exists: questioning the very existence of the ego by Self-inquiry.

All of these paths take effort. Then what about grace? Grace is the natural flow of the Spirit into and through the mind and faculties. There is nothing capricious or erratic about it. As Bhagavan said, "Grace is always there; it is only you who have to make yourself receptive to it." It is like sunlight falling on a flower garden. If one bud opens and not another, it is not because of the sun's partiality, but because of the maturity or immaturity of the buds. If the sunlight penetrates one room but not another, it is simply because the doors and windows are open in one and shut in the other.

Why, then, do the *Upanishads* say that the *Atman* chooses whom it will and that the final Realization comes by grace, not by effort? They do so to remove the mistaken idea that the ego-self can continue to exist and attain something called "Realization." In fact, all the ego can do is to immolate itself and be replaced by the realized state of the Spirit, which is ever-present grace. The mind makes efforts to remove obstructions, yet paradoxically that effort itself constitutes final obstruction. We must carefully watch the desire for Realization, which can become an impediment, for it implies there is a someone to achieve something. At the end of all efforts, the mind must keep still and allow grace to flow unimpeded. That, however, is the hardest thing of all for it to do.

On the devotional path, with its admonition to reverence, desire (even the desire for Realization), and the inflated idea that the ego can attain Self-knowledge, we must cultivate the attitude of being true servants of God, doing everything for love alone with no thought of reward. Those who ask for rewards are merchants, not lovers.

The impossibility of achieving Realization when there is no one to achieve it explains why a guru will never answer the question, "When will I attain Realization?" The question implies the false assumption that: "There is an individual me; when will it cease to exist?" The guru realizes the ultimate truth that, "The unreal does not exist and the Real never ceases to exist." This does not mean that the unreal ego will cease to be at a certain time, but that it does not exist now, has never existed, and never could. Therefore, if you question whether you can attain Realization or whether your destiny enables you to be realized in this lifetime, such an attitude serves as an obstruction to the Realization itself. Such questions assert the temporary existence of the unreal. Similarly, if you assert that you cannot attain Realization in this lifetime, you are preventing yourself from doing so by postulating the existence of a "you" who cannot attain.

And yet, paradoxically, we create an impediment when we assert that we do not have to make any effort, citing the pretext that since "the unreal does not exist and the Real never ceases to exist," we are That now and therefore do not need to strive to become That. While it sounds plausible, we have created an impediment because it is the pseudo-self, the illusory unreal, saying it. The master can say that there is nothing to achieve because one is That already; the disciple cannot. Bhagavan would sometimes say that "asking the way to Realization is like being at Tiruvannamalai and asking how to get there." That, however, should not be the attitude of the devotee, who is expected to make effort, even while appreciating the paradox that there is no one to make it. In the same way, Bhagavan could say that for the realized person, there is no guru-disciple relationship, but add that for the disciple, the relationship is a real and important one.

Disciples must make effort, but they also must remember that effort can never attain the final goal, since the one who makes the effort must dissolve, leaving only Spirit, the true Self. Spirit replaces the illusory ego-self when the latter has removed the obstructions, and that requires grace. Spirit flows into the vacuum that remains when the ego-self dissolves; doing so is the "choice" which the Spirit makes. However, one must create the vacuum by removing the obstructions.

Glossary

Advaita: Nondualism; school of Indian Philosophy, which declares there is no difference between the individual soul and the Supreme Reality.
Advaitin: One who accepts the principles of nonduality.
Ajnana: Ignorance; nescience. Lack of knowledge of the nature of Reality or the Self.
Anatta: Without substance; not-self.
Annamalai: Tamil name for the Arunachala mountain.
Arhat: An enlightened one or holy one, according to *Hinayana* Buddhism. In contrast to the term *bodhisattva* of the *Mahayana* school; the *bodhisattva* wishes to free all beings, while the *arhat*

strives to gain his own salvation.

Arjuna: One of the five Pandava brothers in the epic the *Mahabharata*. Arjuna was taught the highest truth by Krishna in the portion of the *Mahabharata* called the *Bhagavad Gita*.

Arunachala: "Red Mountain" or "Hill of Light." The Sanskrit name for *Annamalai*, the sacred mountain in Tamil Nadu, South India.

Arunachala Aksharamanamalai: "Marital Garland of Letters to Arunachala." One hundred and eight joyful verses spontaneously composed by Maharshi, and often sung by devotees as they walked around the Arunachala Hill.

Ashram: Hermitage; establishment that grows up around a Sage or Guru.

Atma (Atman): Self; the Ultimate Reality which the individual is identical with.

Avidya: Ignorance; nescience.

Bhagavad Gita: The sixth book of the great Indian epic poem the *Mahabharata*, in which the great warrior Arjuna receives fundamental teachings concerning the highest reality from Krishna.

Bhakti: Love; devotion to God.

Bhakti Marga: The spiritual path of realizing the Absolute through love and devotion.

Bodhisattva: One who seeks Buddhahood but renounces complete entry into *nirvana* until all beings are liberated.

Brahmajnana: Knowledge (Realization) of *Brahman*, the Supreme Reality.

Brahman: The Supreme Reality; the Absolute.

Darshan: To have sight of; vision of; especially of saints and sages.
Deepavali: The "Festival of Lights"; a holiday observed throughout India.
Diamond Sutra: One of the great Buddhist scriptures that illustrates how all phenomenal appearances are not intrinsically real, but are the projections of one's own mind.
Dvaitic: That which pertains to *dvaita*; dualism; duality. The philosophical principle which states that God and the individual soul are always separate and real.

Gita: The *Bhagavad Gita*.
Guna(s): Quality; attribute; the characteristics of *Prakriti* or primal nature that underlie all manifestation—*sattva, rajas*, and *tamas* (purity, activity, and inertia).
Guru: Spiritual master; preceptor. One who removes the darkness of ignorance.

Hermetic: A Greek word meaning magical, alchemical, hard to understand, or obscure.
Hinayana: The "lesser vehicle." A term referring to the *Theravada* school of Buddhism, which holds one's own Liberation as the supreme goal rather than the Liberation of all beings.

Ishwara: God; the Supreme Being in manifestation as the entire world.

Janaka: The enlightened king of Videha; father of Sita and father-in-law of Rama, whose life is narrated in the epic work,

the *Ramayana*.
Jivanmukta: One who is fully Liberated, even while alive.
Jnana: Knowledge of the Self; the highest wisdom.
Jnana Marga: The spiritual path of realizing the Absolute through Knowledge.
Jnani: A Sage; one who has realized the Self.

Karma: Action; work; deeds; also the accumulated effect of deeds.
Karma Marga: The spiritual path of realizing the Absolute through selfless action.
Karthikai: Tamil month in which the celebration of the Deepam festival takes place.
Krishna: Name of a divine incarnation, whose exploits are narrated in the great epic, the *Mahabharata,* and in the *Bhagavata-Purana*. In his later life, Krishna befriends the Pandava brothers, especially Arjuna, and reveals to him the great teachings embodied in the *Bhagavad Gita*.

Mahabharata: The great spiritual epic of India. A narrative of the battle between two powerful, related families, which portrays the triumph of truth over evil. Book Six contains the *Bhagavad Gita*, one of the most important Indian philosophical texts.
Mahayana: The Great Vehicle; one of the two main schools of Buddhism. The follower of the *Mahayana* seeks to attain Enlightenment for the sake of the welfare of all beings, rather than just for himself.
Mantra: A sacred word or phrase of spiritual significance and power.

Marathi: The language spoken by people in the Indian state of Maharastra.
Marga: Path; way or approach.
Maya: The principle of appearance; illusion; the power inherent in *Brahman* by which it manifests the world (not ultimately real).
Milarepa: The famous yogi and saint of Tibet (1025-1135) known for his great austerities and profound teachings of Liberation, through the medium of song.
Moksha: Liberation; spiritual freedom; the ultimate goal of human life.
Mouna: Silence; the inexpressible.

Nirvana: Liberation; perfection.

Pandava: Belonging to the family of Pandava's, referred to in the epic the *Mahabharata*.
Prakriti: Primal nature; the phenomenon of *Maya*.
Pranayama: Regulation or control of the breath; one of the eight aspects of *Raja Yoga*.
Prarabdha: That part of one's karma to be worked out in this lifetime.

Ram (Rama): A name for God; usually refers to Rama, who was the King of Ayodhya, and is considered to be a divine incarnation.
Ramayana: The epic story of Rama, who is considered to be a divine incarnation. It was originally written in Sanskrit by the Sage Valmiki. The *Ramayana* is widely venerated in India and Southeast Asia.

Sadguru: The true guru, who is one with the Divine.
Sadhana: Self-effort; spiritual discipline; practice as a means toward Liberation.
Sadhu: A monk or ascetic who has renounced home in the quest for Liberation.
Samadhi: Absorption; deep spiritual contemplation. A state beyond expression and above all thought; beyond the states of waking, dreaming, and deep sleep.
Sannyasi (sannyasin): One who has renounced the world and lives without possessions solely for the purpose of attaining Liberation.
Sanskrit: The ancient language of India, developed over centuries. It was perfected to express spiritual and philosophical truths. It remains the sacred language of Hinduism, since most major spiritual texts were composed in Sanskrit.
Satchitananda (Sat-Chit-Ananda): Being-Consciousness-Bliss.
Satya Yuga: The Golden Age; first of the four ages or cycles of the world.
Shiva: Auspicious; a name for God in his role as destroyer of ignorance.
Shraddha: Belief; faith; an inner attitude reflecting earnestness of purpose.
Subhuti: One of the ten great disciples of the Buddha.
Sutra: Aphorism; concise statements that usually require a commentary for understanding.
Swami: A respectful mode of address that precedes the name of a monk or renunciate. Sometimes follows the name of a spiritual teacher or holy person.

Tamasic: Darkness; one of the three primal qualities (*gunas*); the principle of inertia and dullness.
Tamil: A South Indian language and the earliest branch of the four Dravidian languages. It is not related to the Indo-Aryan languages of which Sanskrit is based.
Tantra: A spiritual practice that involves symbolic ritual, *mantras*, *mudras*, and *mandalas* (symbolic diagrams); the philosophical approach centered around divine energy and creative power.
Tantric: A practitioner of *tantra*; pertaining to the practice of *tantra*.
Tapas: Austerity; concentrated discipline; intense spiritual practice undertaken for the purpose of spiritual attainment.
Tathagata: A title for the Buddha meaning "one who has come and gone." It refers to one who has attained supreme Enlightenment.
Tukaram: A Marathi saint and poet who lived from 1608-1649. His songs enjoyed great popularity among the common people as well as the educated class.

Upadesa Saram: "The Essence of Instruction." Thirty verses composed by Ramana Maharshi, which comprise the spiritual teachings given to the Rishis of Daruka Forest, by Lord *Shiva*.
Upanishad(s): The highest philosophical teachings of *Vedanta*, which form the final portion of the *Veda*.

Vasanas: Latent tendencies or impressions that cling to the individual.
Vasishta: A famous sage and author of the *Rigveda*. His in-

structions to Rama form the basis of the great philosophical work, *Yoga Vasishta*.

Veda(s): The oldest sacred teachings of Indian Literature. *Rig*, *Sama*, *Yajur*, and *Atharva* comprise the four parts of this extensive scripture.

Vedanta: The "end" or consummation of the *Vedas*; based on the teachings in the *Upanishads,* which states the nature of *Brahman* or Reality.

Vedic: That which applies to the *Veda* tradition.

Vichara: Inquiry into the nature of the Self.

Vidura: The chief minister and half-brother of King Dhritarashtra and King Pandu of the *Mahabharata*.

Vishnu: All-pervading; a name for God in his role as preserver of the universe.

Yoga: Union; a spiritual process or discipline leading to oneness with the Divine.

Yoga Vasishta: The spiritual teachings given by Sage Vasishta to Rama. His instructions form the great philosophical work, *Yoga Vasishta*.

Yogi: One who follows or has mastered the path of Yoga.

Yudhishthira: The eldest of the five Pandava brothers, known for his wisdom and righteousness.

Yuga(s): A term referring to one of the four ages or cycles of the world. The four ages are: the Golden Age (*Satya* or *Krita*), the Silver Age (*Treta*), the Bronze Age (*Dvapara*), and the Iron Age (*Kali*).

InnerDirections Publishing is the imprint of the Inner Directions Foundation—a nonprofit organization dedicated to exploring authentic *pathways to awakening* to one's essential nature, in the spirit of Self-inquiry.

Our distinctive selection of book, video, and audio titles reflect clear and direct approaches to realizing *That* which is eternal and infinite within us. These publications reflect the nondualistic ground from which religions and spiritual traditions arise—the infinite consciousness that lies at the heart of all.

To request a catalog of publications, or to find out how you can help sponsor an important book project, call, write, or e-mail:

Inner Directions
P.O. Box 130070
Carlsbad, CA 92013

Tel: 760 599-4075
Fax: 760 599-4076
Orders: 800 545-9118

E-mail: mail@InnerDirections.org
Website: www.InnerDirections.org